PUBLIC SPEAKING

Leadership Guide to Use Storytelling Method in Your Communication to Gain Recognition and Influence People

(How to Speak in Front of an Audience Without Fear)

Carmine Weissman

Published by Rob Miles

© **Carmine Weissman**

All Rights Reserved

Public Speaking: Leadership Guide to Use Storytelling Method in Your Communication to Gain Recognition and Influence People (How to Speak in Front of an Audience Without Fear)

ISBN 978-1-989990-21-6

All rights reserved. No part of this guide may be reproduced in any form without permission in writing from the publisher except in the case of brief quotations embodied in critical articles or reviews.

Legal & Disclaimer

The information contained in this book is not designed to replace or take the place of any form of medicine or professional medical advice. The information in this book has been provided for educational and entertainment purposes only.

The information contained in this book has been compiled from sources deemed reliable, and it is accurate to the best of the Author's knowledge; however, the Author cannot guarantee its accuracy and validity and cannot be held liable for any errors or omissions. Changes are periodically made to this book. You must consult your doctor or get professional medical advice before using any of the suggested remedies, techniques, or information in this book.

Upon using the information contained in this book, you agree to hold harmless the Author from and against any damages, costs, and expenses, including any legal fees potentially resulting from the application of any of the information provided by this guide. This disclaimer applies to any damages or injury caused by the use and application, whether directly or indirectly, of any advice or information presented, whether for breach of contract, tort, negligence, personal injury, criminal intent, or under any other cause of action.

You agree to accept all risks of using the information presented inside this book. You need to consult a professional medical practitioner in order to ensure you are both able and healthy enough to participate in this program.

Table of Contents

INTRODUCTION 1

CHAPTER 1: BELIEVABLITY AND CREDIBILITY 4

CHAPTER 2: THE WHO 6

CHAPTER 3: VARUN'S STORY - BUNCH OF EXCUSES 9

CHAPTER 4: THE NATURE OF THE BEAST: PUBLIC SPEAKING AND STAGE FRIGHT 14

CHAPTER 5: WHY PUBLIC SPEAKING IS IMPORTANT 20

CHAPTER 6: OVERCOMING THE PAST 24

CHAPTER 7: POSTURE 39

CHAPTER 8: TREAT THEM AS YOU WOULD LIKE TO BE TREATED 49

CHAPTER 9: LOSING YOUR PUBLIC SPEAKING VIRGINITY . 57

CHAPTER 10: WHY DO YOU NEED TO OVERCOME YOUR FEAR? 67

CHAPTER 11: FIND YOUR NICHE 71

CHAPTER 12: OVERCOMING THE ANXIETY 76

- **CHAPTER 13: YOURSELF** 85
- **CHAPTER 14: BODY OF THE SPEECH: GET TO THE POINT AND STAY FOCUSED** 91
- *CHAPTER 15:* **BECOME A 'PERFECT PRESENTER'** 104
- **CHAPTER 16: HOW TO BE CONFIDENT ON STAGE** 120
- **CHAPTER 17: HOW TO SEAT YOUR AUDIENCE** 124
- **CHAPTER 18: METHODS OF COMMUNICATION IN PUBLIC SPEAKING** 126
- **CHAPTER 19: WHY HOW TO MAKE MONEY SPEAKING IS UNIQUE** 132
- **CHAPTER 20: MY (BAD) EXPERIENCE WITH PUBLIC SPEAKING** 143
- **CHAPTER 21: APPLYING THE S.U.C.C.E.S.S ACRONYM** 151
- **CHAPTER 22: MAINTAIN YOUR FOCUS ON THE SUBJECT MATTER, NOT THE AUDIENCE** 163
- **CHAPTER 23: PUBLIC SPEAKING IS EASY WHEN YOU KNOW WHAT TO SAY!** 168
- **CHAPTER 24: PERSUASIVE SPEAKING** 175
- **CONLUSION** 197

Introduction

As far back as I can remember, there has always been two kinds of people when it comes to speaking in public. You have the person who thrives the moment they get on stage. It is like a light bulb is turned on and their whole face just lights up. They seem to have this special superpower that has them controlling the crowd and swaying them in the exact direction they want them to go.

Then you have the other kind of people... the ones who suddenly become paralyzed at the prospect of going on stage. I don't know what category you belong to. Are you looking to overcome your stage fright? Or maybe you are just looking for a leg up in an industry that requires you to be unique, but demands that you deliver the same level of excellence in service as everyone. It can get difficult to tow the line between being yourself and abiding by the unspoken rules of a profession that you are not very familiar with in the first place.

This book is about freeing you from the confines of your fears and getting you to that point where public speaking is no longer a sweat-inducing event. Rather, it becomes a podium that gives you a powerful voice; one that you could use to instigate change. And if that feels like too much pressure, you can simply use this book to learn how to become a better communicator. After all, there will be a point in your life where you would be addressing more than two people at the same time and just in case you didn't know it, that is the starting point of public speaking.

Each chapter in this book begins with a powerful quote to set the tone for what you are about to read. It goes on to give practical analysis of problems or issues encountered by people who have attempted to do public speaking. It then provides actionable solutions to those problems. At the end of each chapter, you would find a task or two. These tasks are designed to help you grow as a speaker. You owe it to yourself to perform those tasks.

I hope that this book is everything you want it to be. That said, let us begin!

Chapter 1: Believablity And Credibility

What makes you believable? If you speak, do you think that you have automatic credibility? I am sorry to say, that not only do you not have instant credibility, but there may be some people that will never believe you. But, if you believe your message, if you are sold on your product, if you sincerely feel as if what you have to say is important, then you will be able to convince many.

So what about it, are you sure that you believe what you are saying or selling? When you believe it, you have a certain believability that is absent when you are doubtful. It is noticeable. If you do not believe in what you are speaking about, maybe you should do some self examination at the very onset of this book. If you do not believe in yourself, and speak with enthusiasm, confidence and control, your audience will most likely not believe you.

Be convinced and convicted about what you are saying.

So, just what is it that you are speaking about? What is the message you are revealing? How important is it that your audience hear it? Is it a message that is vital and informative, or is it a message that is entertaining and light hearted? Are you trying to sell a product or an idea, or are you just trying to make them laugh? Decide now what you are speaking about, then you will be able to understand the kind of speech you will need to use.

Chapter 2: The Who

Who am I talking to (or some purists prefer **to whom am I speaking)?** Audiences might be generally friendly, unfriendly (sometimes hostile), cautious, open, closed, indifferent and so on, for a variety of reasons. These reasons can be cultural, personal, religious, political, racial, educational….The list is long.

Hence getting to know something about your audience is essential. You can do this by asking other speakers who have spoken to the audience, or try to do some form of audience surveying in advance. Find out about their likes, dislikes, values, beliefs, as well as current information on what might have been happening in their town, city, community, village or region. I remember once speaking to a community, and in talking about a serious problem pointed out how **lucky** they were in not having that type of problem in their community. Some audience members were quick to disagree with me. I realized then that my credibility was shot in an instant because I hadn't upgraded my research to the most recent facts and events about this community. Of course, following that **faux pas** I had to work really hard to rebuild credibility--regain audience's confidence in how much I knew about them and what I was talking about.

Ignorance of your audience can be a real turn off. Avoid coming across as someone who is disinterested or just couldn't care to learn about them.

On some occasions you might have to expend a lot of energy trying to win over your audience, and this is where building common ground through such areas as likes and interests, is quite useful. Using universal appeals such as peace and love, hope and dreams, can also bring positive results. On the same note, some audience members can come across as really hostile during Q&A sessions. Defuse any conflict with calm and patience.

Knowing who you are….

Of course, this brings up the point that relating to your audience, which includes sharing things in common, means that you have to have a keen sense of who you are. What are your likes and dislikes, your interests? What's important and of value to you? What of your experiences would you want to share with others present?

I have spoken to some young adults who don't have the faintest idea about their hobbies, their passions, or what's happening in current local and global news. Bringing a strong sense of who you are to your speech raises your confidence and energy levels and helps you connect more directly or **build rapport** with your audience.

Getting in touch with yourself takes time, longer for some than for others. For the young adult it's a known stage for searching, discovery and growth. Remember, just like everything else, it takes effort and facing challenges to get to know who you are and what you are about.

Chapter 3: Varun's Story - Bunch Of Excuses

A friend of mine, Varun Khatri wanted his son, Aditya Khatri to learn public speaking. The son was around 12 yrs. Old. He refused to pay attention to what his father would say. Every attempt to reason out the importance of Public Speaking fell on deaf ears. The father was left alone with his arguments, with a list of excuses bundled and showered upon him by his son.

Oh Dad! I have unit tests...

Oh Dad! I have my subjective assessments....

Oh Dad! I have to make a model for ....
Oh Dad! Lots of homework...
Oh Dad! I am watching my favourite show...pleeeaaseee....
Oh Dad! It's playtime now...
Chill Dad!...

Although, Varun understood the stress Aditya or any child had to go through in their school, he also understood one thing- If Aditya does not start honing his skills now, not only would he regret it later but it would also be very difficult for him to cope with the competitive environment outside after he finished school, entered college and future prospects. Summer Vacations also brought in their set of challenges with them. Not only was there a lot of homework to be completed and submitted, exams were also in the pipeline after the schools re-open. Even if he forced the child to sit down with him during the vacations, that was not enough.

He deciphered Public Speaking as a skill that needed to be continually honed and practised over a longer duration.

One day, the entire family was at the dinner table. Varun with his wife, daughter and son. The dinner had all the favourite items of all the family members. They started with the salad round first. It had onions, cucumber, tomatoes in it. Everyone in the family picked a slice each of all the ingredients from the plate except for Aditya. He chose only onion and cucumber. His mother was furious on seeing this. She started scolding him for not eating tomatoes and started citing the reasons for having them. Varun noticed his son not heeding his mother's advice. He was quick enough to pick up this opportunity and intervened between the two. He said, "Ok Shobha, If Aditya proves it to us that he is right, we will not force him to eat tomatoes anymore. He can take his time to think over the arguments by the time we finish our dinner. Right Aditya?" Aditya pleased at not being forced to eat tomatoes, immediately nodded his head in agreement.

After dinner ended, the entire family gathered to listen to what Aditya had to say. Aditya started like this ....

Oh Papa, Oh Mama, you know very well that I hate tomatoes. I agree it has a beautiful red colour and wears a lovely green crown on its head. It is used in making the gravy tasty, makes nice meat and is also eaten raw. It is also a panacea to many diseases. It contains many nutrients. It prevents us from a disease called scurvy. Not only this, it helps to remove iron deficiency and strengthens our teeth and bones.

Not only this, my elder sister uses it to get beautiful everyday as if she has to win a beauty contest. As I am already consuming it in so many different ways, I do not believe that I will have any deficiency if I do not eat it raw.

(Ref Video: https://www.youtube.com/watch?v=U5iTxB4354s)

I am sure, as a parent you must be curious to know if he started eating tomatoes or not. Trust me friends, he did. That also on his own. No one in the family compelled him but when he had himself cited so many points in favour of its nutritional value and realised the futility of his refusal, who would not start eating it? It is just that you need to be patient the moods of a growing up adult. As they say, strike only when the iron is hot **but GENTLY this time** as we are dealing with soft and sensitive minds. This is what Varun did too.

Chapter 4: The Nature Of The Beast:

Public Speaking And Stage Fright

To start off, let's give me some background. I'm not just some random chap off the street – I've been on stage before, several times, from elementary to high school, and stage fright's a familiar phenomenon for me.

I've delivered a few speeches, all of them extemporaneously; I've never been one for preparing a speech beforehand, it just isn't my thing. I can assure you that, in terms of this, I know what I'm talking about.

Now, let us define the term 'public speaking'. Cribbing a few definitions off the internet leads to the following:

Public speaking is the act of making speeches, most often to audiences of some numbers, for purposes of information, entertainment, or persuasion.

Strangely, it's also ranked rather highly among a few studies as to what people fear. Rather strange, when all it involves is getting up, talking to a few people, and then sitting back down.

Well, all right, it's not **that** simple, but that's really what the whole business boils down to. Strange how a simple thing can make jelly out of the knees of so many. It's not unjustified, though; that fear mainly stems from a phenomenon very closely associated with public speaking: stage fright, which we'll presently just call 'the fright'.

And the fright takes its form in the many fears that plague the prospective public speaker. He may fear that he'll screw up so badly that he'll make a complete and utter fool of himself in public.

Or she may doubt her capability and hence think herself incapable of delivering a good performance. Or the speaker may be pressured by thinking that she needs to put out a good performance, in order to avoid embarrassment. Or the speaker could be self-conscious regarding manner and appearance, among other things.

Some of these are valid concerns, true enough. The oddest thing about public speaking is that, by itself, the act is a very familiar thing. Unless there are mitigating circumstances, most of those who speak publicly also speak in everyday life, to an audience of one or two or just a little more.

The trouble really comes when this familiar thing is dropped into a greatly unfamiliar milieu: instead of just speaking to one person or a few about anything relevant that comes to mind, one speaks to an audience of substantial numbers about a particular subject, which the speaker may or may not know anything of.

And it's certainly possible that the audience itself may be unfamiliar. In some cases, this may work to some advantage: An audience that does not know the speaker can miss some personal cues regarding nervousness, and pass them off as something else.

However, in most other cases the unfamiliarity more often works against the speaker, as he doesn't know the audience and thus may feel less comfortable and far more awkward for it. And, if there's social differences, the self-consciousness could very well come into play and go about making trouble; it can get rather difficult to deliver a speech if the entire audience is in white tie, while the speaker's in jeans and a shirt.

The reason for all the fright is that, unlike so many other types of performance art, there is nothing at all between the speaker and the audience.

The speaker isn't acting (deliberately) or playing an instrument, but is instead using only his own voice, with or without the assistance of a microphone.

Barring an equipment failure, any missteps made during the speech are entirely the speaker's own. The burden, thus, is entirely on the speaker, with not much else to shift it to.

Now, the degree of fright always varies, depending on certain things. The audience is a factor — some may fare better with audiences at a thousand or more, and turn into jelly at twenty or fewer.

Some may feel more comfortable with people of a different social class, and be less confident at speaking to peers. Others may find it more difficult with friends than with anonymous people or mere acquaintances. Some settings may cause more fright than others, unfamiliar locations and audiences the most of all.

There's a great number of other possible things that can cause the fright, far too many to easily list, but the ones stated above are generally the main factors.

Chapter 5: Why Public Speaking Is Important

We really can't overstate just how important public speaking is. We all must speak in front of a group of people at least a few times in our lives. For others, it is something they will need to practice on a regular basis if they want to be successful in their careers. Wherever you happen to fall on the spectrum, mastering public speaking is a valuable skill to have.

For many career paths, being a confident and skilled public speaker is a sign of leadership. Businesses are always looking for leaders, and they will reward you handsomely if you can show that you have the skills to lead, persuade and inspire. So if you can show that you can give effective business presentations or express yourself well in management and team meetings, upper management will take notice. This can lead to promotions and added opportunities for your career that you wouldn't have otherwise.

In your personal life, being an effective public speaker can also open up doors of opportunity to help achieve things for your children's schools, your church, your favorite charity and more. You can have the personal satisfaction of knowing that you are looked upon as a leader, and that you have the ability to be persuasive and cause others to act to help achieve goals that are personally meaningful to you.

Being an effective public speaker will also make you a more confident person and raise your self esteem. These are huge factors in helping you to be a successful and fulfilled individual. Once you are able to master the art of public speaking, you will have the confidence and skills to address audiences of all types on various subjects that matter to you. No matter what the occasion happens to be, you will be able to walk into a room knowing that you can make a difference.

Overcoming your fears about public speaking will also ease your mind of so much anxiety, stress and self doubt. This alone is worth all of the effort you put into public speaking and being able to deliver a good speech. When we can conquer our fears, we can leave behind so much stress and worry and start to concentrate on the positive aspects of life. This has a huge effect on both our mental and physical well being.

As you can see there are numerous benefits to becoming an effective public speaker for both your professional and personal life. It is well worth the time to learn how to conquer your fears and become a skilled speaker. Keep this in mind as you are going through this process. Remember that all of the time and effort that you are putting in are well worth it. This will help you follow through and persist through the difficult and challenging times. Picture in your mind giving the speech of your life and all the positive responses you will receive. Visualize the confident speaker you are about to become and how many doors this will open for you.

Chapter 6: Overcoming The Past

So you may have screwed up, or gone through a painful experience at some stage in your life and you've vowed and declared, "Never doing that again". It was humiliating, confidence-zapping and something you would rather forget about FOREVER!

Am I making you feel worse about it all? Good.

That means deep down you would

LIKE TO DO SOMETHING ABOUT IT

But have no idea

WHERE TO START or ...

Perhaps you've never uttered a word on stage, in public, in front of friends or work mates.

The thought of speaking in public sends cold shivers down your spine. Great.

Let's call this

GROUND ZERO.

The good news is you are not alone.
When I searched for the number one fear in many countries, it aced it for me right there and then.
This book WAS a good idea and would be helpful to many people.
What are people most afraid of?
A terrorist attack?
Getting shot during a robbery or break-in?
Dying broke?
Getting sick and unable to afford medical care?
The TV breaking down on a Monday night?
Being alone?
HOWEVER
According to Google
The official
NUMBER ONE FEAR?
SPEAKING IN PUBLIC.
So why would so many PEOPLE fear PUBLIC SPEAKING so much that it would be on the top of the list?

Good question. Throughout this book, I would like to dispel your fears, both real and irrational. Let's get rid of your classic reasons/excuses for not having a go.

Let me share a quick story about my 'terrible' experiences speaking in public and how speaking turned out to be one of the great joys of life.

As a practiced and experienced speaker, I now truly find it easy to stand up in front of people and speak - the larger the audience the better!

It wasn't always that way.

My nick name at school was 'Mumbles' based on the classic Dick Tracey cartoon character. Remember the one with the funny mouth who simply mumbled his way through each episode?

I spoke so fast and jumbled with my squeaky voice that few people could understand me.

The standard response from most people was 'Would you say that again, this time so I can understand you?' or 'Hey slow down a bit!'

Like most things in life, you jump one of two ways when there is something going on with you.

You either stay that way and resent it all your life OR you actually do something about it.

You no doubt have witnessed, perhaps first hand, how cruel kids at school can be when you are not 'perfect' and the 'mumbles' tag hurt pretty good.

I eventually got the mumbling thing sorted by learning to open my mouth a little more when speaking.

Then it was onto the habit of rapid fire delivery.

I sounded a lot like the voice over guy at the end of a radio or television commercial with a long list of terms and conditions applying!

I talked myself into thinking it was because I had a quick brain. Yeah right!

It was a slog but eventually, all the effort started to show results. My speech eventually came under some sort of control. Then low and behold, I ended up following a media career which started on radio as a music jock. Me a DJ saying stuff on the radio? 20 years as a news anchor too!

Luckily, I had a genuine determination to speak well. That simply meant speaking clearly enough for listeners to understand what I was saying…

THE FIRST TIME!

So I started to really work at it. One day when I was about 22 and on radio, an opportunity came up to 'MC' a fashion parade on stage. It was a charity gig that was being filmed. They obviously had someone pull out at the last minute and I became the substitute!

It was a case of the old saying "what doesn't kill you makes you stronger"

To say I was terrified, didn't come close to how I really felt. It was literally the next day.

They sort of begged me to do it out of their own desperation, so I said (gulp) YES.

Although I looked OK, dressed in a nice suit with a crisp shirt and cool necktie, I was seriously shaking in my shoes.

The introduction?

Well I went with the basic "Hello everyone and welcome to the fashion parade!" I acknowledged the sponsors and the organizers of the show.

Got through that OK- then onto the business.

I had to do the introduction for each designer and had palm cards to read about the individual pieces as the gorgeous models paraded and strutted their stuff. It was the early eighties with big shoulder pads, big hair and high shoes!

I got through that part, but I was terrible!

Fumbling, bumbling and of course had the palm cards mixed up at some stage and was reading the wrong one for the outfit on stage - your classic screw up! However the co-host covered for me well. She knew her stuff and carried on like nothing was wrong.

The whole experience taught me
MANY
BIG
LESSONS!

Much of it was learned on stage - not a great place to get an education in front of a whole bunch of people who knew more about what was going on than I did.

The most valuable lessons of all were learned watching the playback of the video. That gave me a chance to break down and analyze what went right and the whole bunch of stuff that wasn't so good.

From there, I really got the taste for it and started to create other opportunities to be out front and on the microphone.

So what am I saying to anyone who has read this far?

If you really WANT to overcome your fear of public speaking, take heart. YOU CAN.

Your reasons for doing this may be to gain more confidence in front of people.

It may be simply for the sheer thrill of conquering a REAL FEAR.

Or it might be to advance yourself both personally and professionally.

In this book I WILL GUIDE YOU through EACH AND EVERY STEP.

The single biggest hold-back
for most people is FEAR.

What you are fearful about is a list of boogie-man thoughts that just seem to jump into your brain even at the mere mention of speaking in public.

What would I talk about?

What would I say?

I don't have anything to talk about that other people would be interested in?

I'm just not confident enough to speak in front of other people, let alone a group, or God forbid, a large audience at a seminar!
No way am I getting up there. **People will think I'm no good.** Where would I start?
And a whole bunch of **"what if's"**
What if I forget what I was supposed to say?
What if I say something stupid and they laugh at me?
What if they don't like me?
What if ... what if ... what if...
What if I show you how to discover that there are valuable things inside of you that you could say? Probably lots of them.
What if I show you a three-step, ridiculously easy-to-follow method, that helps you discover and guides you on what to say?
What if I show you a dead-easy way to plan your first public speech?
What if I show you a fail-safe way to muster the confidence to actually do this?

What if I show you how to start strongly without even knowing it?

What if I show you and guide you to becoming a successful and sought after public speaker?

And what if I could guarantee you that if you follow this 'anyone can do it' method of learning the inside secrets to being a public speaker you will nail it. (Especially those of you who have a major fear of even trying)

Sound good?

It's true.

There is a whole series of insider secrets that I reveal

throughout this book.

If you follow them and have the courage to practice a little, you will at some stage step up to the plate and actually deliver a neat, heartfelt speech that will cause you to thrill YOURSELF!

And that, ladies and gentlemen is a journey worth taking - for YOU.

If you are at ground zero as a speaker, the challenge you need to get a handle on is to actually make a start.

In my simple way of thinking, the most important part of any project is to just start.

It could mean grabbing a piece of paper and pen and just writing down one thing you could talk about. **It mentally breaks the ice.**

But where do I start?

If you were a coach teaching someone from ground zero how to play basketball where would you start?

Would you try to teach them how to drive inside the defense and lay it up?

Would you teach them how to dribble, feign a pass, go round the taller player and take a three point shot from outside the key?

Probably not!

Most likely you would start with the basics - **correct?**

Speaking is just the same.

I recall reading a piece about how to teach young kids to play golf. It started with **placing the ball on the green and tapping it into the hole** from

short distances. Which, to a kid, is hitting the target.

There is an immediate feeling of success.

It's not likely a kid would want to persist with golf if you started with a whopping driver and tried to teach the little tacker how to smack the ball 250 yards down the middle of the fairway.

Same with public speaking.

If you are just starting out, you want to establish a successful track record right from the get go … Correct? Get the feeling of being able to do this.

Start out with a reasonably small expectation.

Oh here we go again with

"I DON'T KNOW WHAT TO SAY"

coming up in your mind.

Stop right there!

Take a mental breath - there ARE things you CAN talk about. You just haven't thought of them yet. We'll get there soon enough.

But first let's go back in time a little bit.

Do you remember when you were learning to ride a bike? That magic moment when the person guiding you actually let go of the bike without you knowing and you were in fact riding by yourself?

What a thrill.

Speaking has a magic formula to success that is known by every practiced speaker.

When you learn this simple but universal structure, it will open up a whole new world for you. There is magic in simplicity.

So here is the magic formula for becoming a competent and confident public speaker.

There is an OPEN.

There is the BODY.

There is a CLOSE.

No matter what level you are as a speaker, it is the same basic formula.

That's it????? You must be kidding me?

You may have thought it was going to be some grand secret formula but not so. As I said, there is magic in simplicity - that's why it works so well.

It's the one thing you really need to 'get'.

So if you get nothing else from this book, please get this...

You CAN do this.

You CAN speak in front of others.

You CAN connect with an audience.

When you SPEAK FROM THE HEART there are no mistakes.

Even if your head is screaming at you at this point "No, no, no that's too hard ... I couldn't bear to get up in front of people and say something, let alone make a speech." you CAN do it.

Let that thought just sit for a minute. Humor me that you COULD at some point possibly speak in front of others. OK?

Remember, if you are like most people, you do something every day in your job or your hobby or your special interest that would make others shudder at the thought.

So let's start the three-step

dance with the first bit first ... The **OPEN.**

Chapter 7: Posture

The Importance of Posture

It's all very well and good breathing properly and speaking articulately, but a great public speaker will usually accompany good vocal skills with a strong posture.

We live in an age where people are very judgmental about appearance, and even in professional situations we often make snap judgments about a person based on how they hold themselves.

Think of the best speakers you know, whether they be old teachers, colleagues from work, sales people or politicians, and think about how they stand when delivering a speech.

Essentially, impressive posture is about bringing the chest up, and the back down. The exercises in this section will help you to do this, by aligning the spine and awakening the chest.

1. Semi-Supine Position

Semi-supine position is a great starting point for working on your posture, as it aligns your spine and neck. It's something that's relaxing, very simple, and incredibly effective if practiced regularly. Some people encourage you to rest your head on a book to achieve an ideal head-neck-back position, but this is up to you to decide as the ideal position varies from person to person. This must be practiced on a hard floor, as every vertebra of your spine needs to feel full contact with the ground.

Lay face up on the floor with your head comfortable and your neck horizontal.

Bend your legs and pull your knees towards your chest gently. Then let them slowly fall, planting your feet firmly on the ground.

Rest your arms, hands palm down, by your sides.

Remain in this position for as long as it takes to feel your back and neck align themselves. I usually find 10 minutes is ideal.

Remember

This position is a great starting point as it aligns your spine and puts your whole body in order. Spend time here to 'check in' with yourself, and notice any aches and pains that might be in your muscles or joints.

It's very easy to let your mind drift off in this position, but don't fall into that trap! It's important to stay focused on your body and your senses. Imagine your spine is a river, with your brain as the source passing messages down to every one of your muscles.

Focus your mind so that the river can flow freely to the extremities of your body, allowing you to wake your muscles up before even having to move them. I recommend listening to relaxing music with this, but it's not essential.

Important

The only point of tension in your whole body should be a tiny amount in your pelvis keeping your legs in position.

Check that you aren't arching your spine by trying to slide your hand under your back, there should be no space between your spine and the floor.

2. Pelvic Lift

This exercise is designed to loosen the back and to get fluid into the vertebrae of your spine, increasing robustness and flexibility:

Lay in semi-supine position and relax into a slow breathing pattern.

As you take a full breath in, raise your pelvis off the ground, forming a bridge from your knees to your neck. Roll each vertebra of your spine up from the ground one at a time, starting with those at the bottom and working your way up until your neck is supporting your weight.

On your out-breath roll back down, starting with your neck and return to semi-supine position.

Repeat for 6 full breaths.

3. Warming the Neck & Spine

This exercise will stretch your neck and back muscles to improve mobility:

From semi-supine position bring up your arms to form a cross shape.

From this position, slowly tilt your legs to the right and lower your right knee to the ground, with your left knee resting above it. As you do so, gently roll your head to the left, and let it rest, as far round as it will comfortably go. Remain in this position for eight full breaths.

After eight breaths, slowly roll your head and legs back into the cross position, before rolling your head to the right, and your legs to the left. Remain here for a further eight full breaths.

Roll back through the cross position and alternate sides once more, only this time as you bring your legs to the right, keep your right leg bent, and extend your left leg as far as it will go towards your right hand. Hold for eight full breaths.

Perform step 4 on the alternate side, then come back to center.

4. Yogic Cat Position

The cat position is a yoga sequence that greatly improves posture:

Begin on all fours, with your hands directly below your shoulders and your knees directly below your hips.

As you breathe in through your nose, bring your head up and look to the ceiling, and push your stomach down towards the ground.

As you breathe out, curve your spine inwards and bring your head down between your arms as far as it will go. Empty your lungs and try to push yourself further, curving your back and holding in your head.

Repeat the sequence for eight full breaths, and you should feel your spine align itself. Finally drop back onto your feet and rest before you stand again.

5. Forward Bend

This exercise is designed to strengthen and flex your spine, while at the same time engaging your diaphragm and core stomach muscles. Begin with your legs apart about a meter:

Take a deep in-breath and raise your hands up to hold the back of your head (Position One).

Slowly breathe out and bend forward from the stomach, until your head rests between your legs as far as it will comfortably go (Position Two).

Breathe in deeply while in this position, then breathe out and as you do, gently push your head a little further, without straining your neck.

Keep breathing deeply in and out, pushing your head a little further between your legs each time. Do this for eight breaths before coming up to standing.

Position One   Position Two

6. Child Pose, and Rise to Standing

This position is often thought of as a relaxation pose, and indeed many people treat it as a rest after more vigorous work. However, child pose can also be used to focus your mind and be a launch-pad into standing up properly:

Simply drop back from all fours, resting your buttocks on your heels and pointing your toes slightly inwards. Keep your arms held out in front of you (as opposed to the traditional pose, where the arms stay by the sides) and feel the stretch in your biceps and forearms. Breathe deeply, taking as long as you need to become comfortable in the position, and register the effects of the warm up so far on your muscles.

In your own time, slowly push yourself back onto your feet using your hands and arms. Keep your feet shoulder width apart and most importantly don't lift your head, keep it hanging loosely between your knees.

Very gradually lift yourself up in one smooth motion, *keeping your head hanging loose until the very last moment*. Push up with your legs and unroll your spine until you are vertical, and then slowly raise your head.

This method of standing has many benefits over just springing up from the ground. You are able to check in with your body from the ground up, and clear your mind

as you rise to survey your environment.

Chapter 8: Treat Them As You Would Like To Be Treated

Think about it like this: you go for a coffee with a friend, family member or significant other. How would you feel if they spent the entire conversation, or large chunks of it, fidgeting and staring at the ceiling or the floor, and very little of the conversation looking you in the eye, smiling and using facial expressions?

Distant?

Alienated?

Maybe even under-valued.

The same principle applies when speaking to large groups of people as when having a conversation with an individual.

You do not want to appear to treat the audience as if they are not in the room with you, or as if you would rather be elsewhere.

It is generally a good idea to avoid simply rehearsing and delivering the material verbatim without engaging the audience. If you make a conscious effort to speak off-the-cuff, you will be more present in the moment, as opposed to just treating the performance like a rehearsal that happens to be in front of a room full of people.

Speaking off-the-cuff can be daunting to those not used to it, and this was certainly the case for me. My advice would be to **start small**. It could be as simple as commenting that it is one of the biggest crowds you have spoken in front of, or that you are slightly out of your comfort zone with what you are doing, and thanking everyone for attending and bearing with you regardless.

You could jokingly apologise to the compere or certain members of the audience for boring them with some of the same material on more than one occasion, if you are repeating something they have seen you do before.

You could talk about how slippery the stage is and how you would have worn shoes with more grip if you had known.

In general, keep observations and comments light-hearted.

Looking individuals in the eye directly is very important. Many times, I have seen highly skilled speakers who simply stared at the ceiling, the floor, or anywhere but the audience for the duration of their talk. I couldn't help feeling distant from them in these cases, as if I may as well be watching it on a screen.

Making the effort to look people in the eye, even if just sporadically when glancing up from a page or an instrument, seems like such a simple concept, and the last thing I want to do is state the obvious, but it is amazing how few people actually do this.

Some speakers can find eye contact with the audience intimidating or off-putting, which it can be for those who are not used to it, but can become easier with practice as you get more comfortable speaking to audiences. Those who make a point of pushing through this barrier, in baby steps if need be, will reap the rewards, and start to build more camaraderie with whoever may be watching.

One trick which can be very effective is, if possible, to **go unplugged**. That is, speaking without a microphone. I once saw a live poetry performance in which the poet, as soon as he got up on stage, pushed the microphone stand to one side, and did his entire set without it. This added power to his performance, and also freed up both his hands (he did not read from a page) to use expressive gestures, as well as allowing him to move around.

Doing an entire talk or set without a microphone is not necessary. For those with medical issues relating to their voice, or going unplugged for long periods of time without proper vocal training, it may not be advisable. However, if it can be done for even the odd word or sentence, it can be a great crowd-pleaser. It can come across as less artificial, and can make the audience feel a more organic, genuine connection to the speaker.

If the speaker or performer leaves the stage and delivers instead from the area where the audience are, this can also be effective, as it reduces the physical distance between them.

I once saw a live band that played the entirety of their set from the stage, with the exception of one song which they performed unplugged, standing amongst the audience. It was without a doubt the highlight of their performance.

Speakers or performers can generally send a good message of equality by travelling to the stage (or equivalent area) in the first place via the audience area, as opposed to a backstage VIP room, which suggests more disparity.

It is vital that the speaker always remembers to put themselves in the shoes of their audience. If you were listening to a speaker, you would expect them to do their utmost to give you something of real value to make it worth your time, and not merely show an interest in plugging their own products or business. It should also go without saying that a speaker not criticise the audience or put them down in any way.

Something which is greatly important is the personality the speaker exudes. As you become more experienced as a speaker, and your confidence and abilities grow exponentially (which they will the more you do it), do not fall into the trap of letting it go to your head.

Being confident in your abilities and being cocky are not worlds apart. Audiences do not respond well to those with disproportionate egos, and neither would you.

Someone who saw one of my live poetry performances recently said that he thinks I have a modest edge, and encouraged me not to lose that. I absolutely intend not to.

Remember also that your 'window' for connecting with your audience is not confined to the duration of your talk itself.

Before your talk, shake their hands and make them feel welcome.

After your talk, if audience members stay for a few minutes (as some always do), chat to them, thank them for coming, and just get to know them.

Whenever I chat to a speaker or performer who I look up to and have been in awe of, it strikes me how, when it comes down to it, they are just a person, no different from you or I. As a speaker, you want your audience to think this about you. Do not think of yourself as being above them.

Chapter 9: Losing Your Public Speaking Virginity

Imagine you're in a classroom. Who do you think speaks excellently? You may select those who look smart or those who often recite in class. You may think that these people are actually more confident than you think they are. Or perhaps, they are born speakers and you are not.

Well, it may surprise you that they're probably thinking the same thing about you! They may also feel that you are a born speaker and envy you because they have fears in public speaking. Some may have special interests in public speaking, but most people do not know anything about it.

Then again, you may actually be a good speaker without realizing it. It pays to find out by actually doing it and by seeing yourself doing it. You may be just like this student during his first speech in class.

He needed to prepare a long speech. Two weeks before, he had started writing his speech. He could not sleep at night. In fact, the night before his speech, he did not sleep at all. However, when he finally did his speech and saw it on video, he realized that it was not as bad as he expected it to be. He did not experience the usual symptoms of speech anxiety, such as going blank while speaking, or speaking very softly and hearing chuckles in the audience. Through the video, he discovered that he has actually improved in public speaking.

If no video of your speech is available yet, you can watch yourself speak formally in front of a mirror.

Preparing Yourself to Speak

Here are the basic rules of public speaking:

• Gain an understanding of who you are. Discover your own knowledge, capabilities, biases and potentials.

• Gain an understanding of your audience. Ponder upon what the audience wants to hear, what provokes their interest, what they believe in and what they want to know.

• Gain an understanding of the situation. Consider how the setting of the place and other unforeseen factors could affect the way you deliver your speech.

• Anticipate response from the audience. Make sure you have a clear purpose in mind so that the audience will respond in the way you want them to.

• Search for other sources of information. There might be more materials available for you to make your speech more colorful.

• Come up with an argument that is reasonable. Make sure that the purpose of your speech is supported by clear and reliable data to formulate a sound argument.

• Add structure to your message. Organize your ideas so that the audience will not have a hard time following and digesting your ideas.

• Talk directly to your audience. Make sure the language you are using is one that your audience is comfortable with. Consider the occasion in delivering your speech.

• Gain self-confidence through practice. It is only through practice can you effectively present your speech. Master the flow of your presentation by repeatedly rehearsing it. That way, you can have command over your speech.

Becoming a Good Public Speaker

You have probably heard professors give boring and monotonous lectures. Dull presentations clearly point that a lot of people do not give much importance to good speeches. These speakers may even be unaware that they are boring or ineffective because they lack knowledge about the basic characteristics of a good speech. Hence, to prevent this pitfall, you must remember some basic principles.

1. Respect the variety of the audience.

Good speakers do not look down on their audience. They consider the audience as equals. They know that the listeners have different backgrounds; hence communicating to each of them effectively would also entail different methods.

Before actually organizing a speech, you have to take into consideration your audience. Consider such things as age, gender, and cultural backgrounds. What do they know about your topic? What are their beliefs and values? By looking at these factors, you can choose a topic that suits them and style your speech in the way you feel would be most effective.

The whole experience can be more enjoyable if you prepare well for the individual and cultural differences of your audience. For example, will both male and female listeners appreciate the information you will prepare? Would your Hispanic audience be comfortable with the language you're using as much as the Native Americans would? Would some of your comments offend the senior citizens while addressing the younger generation? The more you know about the audience, the better the chances that you will capture their attention and the more you can make your speech fit their situations. They would feel comfortable listening to you and you would have a better interaction with them.

2. Know as much as possible about listening.

Successful communication does not only depend on good speakers; it depends on good listeners as well. It is a two-way process. If the speaker prepares a very polished speech, it would be useless if the audience does not listen. Know also how to "listen" to the gesticulated reactions of your audience. How comfortable or uneasy they look speaks volumes in terms of their interest or comprehension.

3. Organize carefully to improve understanding and recall.

The best presentations are those with interconnected ideas that flow smoothly from one idea to the next. It is effective because the listeners will be able to follow your arguments and will not get confused along the way.

Three parts of a well-organized speech:

• Introduction: Capture the attention of your audience, boost their interest, and give them a background of your topic.

• Body: Start with your main ideas. Keep them organized and support them with visual and verbal aids as much as possible.

• Conclusion: Provide a recap of all your points and join them together in a way that will create an impact on your listeners, making them remember your points.

4. Use language effectively.

Keep it short. The simpler the language you use, the more powerful and interesting your speech will be. Too many words expressing a single idea will only confuse the audience and will make your argument weak. By keeping it short but accurate, your audience will remember what you will say and they will appreciate it.

5. Sound natural and enthusiastic.

The problem with first timers is they either memorize the speech verbatim or rely on too many flashcards for their notes. These can make the speaker sound unnatural. Talk normally to people so they would listen more to you. By being natural and enthusiastic, it would be like discussing a favorite subject with your friends. Basically, avoid putting up a "speaking disguise" when you talk. Treat it like an ordinary conversation with your usual companions.

6. Use high-quality visual aids.

A simple text containing key phrases and pictures is an example of a visual aid. Usually, visual aids (Chapter 10) can be anything that supplements your speech. It will greatly help your listeners to follow the flow of your ideas and to understand them at a faster rate. It also gives credibility to your speech, which makes you feel more relaxed and confident throughout. However, avoid making poor visuals because they become more of a distraction than support. Treat visual preparations with equal importance as the speech preparation itself.

7. Give only ethical speeches.

Accuracy is very important. It would be difficult for your audience to make informed choices if the information you give is false or vague. Research to ensure credibility and clarity. Avoid plagiarism, falsification and exaggeration of your information. Also, when trying to persuade, do not manipulate, deceive, force, or pressure. Develop good arguments through sound logic and concrete evidence. This is ethical persuasion. Once information is falsified, it becomes unethical because it prevents listeners from making informed choices.

Basically, good speakers aim to change the beliefs, values, or attitudes of the audience through clean persuasion.

Chapter 10: Why Do You Need To Overcome Your Fear?

As mentioned in the previous chapter, nowadays it is important that you overcome your fear of speaking in public. In today's society, it is crucial that people be more vocal about what they want and need, or else their voice will go unheard (literally). To motivate you to go on your journey towards self-improvement, here are some benefits to help you overcome your fears and actually be able to deliver an awesome speech in front of a crowd of strangers.

It Will Give Your Self-Confidence a Huge Boost

Sometimes, the primary reason you can't speak in public in the first place is your low self-esteem. Then again, you may have a speech impediment, which you are afraid that it will cause you to embarrass yourself, or you have a negative body image that just the thought of standing in front of a group of total strangers may be terrifying for you. Whatever the reasons, it is critical for you to overcome your fear of public speaking.

You can overcome your fears once you are successful in giving your very first speech. Then you will notice that your confidence will increase significantly, and with this you will be able to start giving speeches more effectively. Just like the old saying, "It's like the gift that keeps on giving!"

You Will Learn How to be More Assertive

Do you consider yourself a "door mat"? In other words, do other people regularly take advantage of you because you cannot defend yourself? If your answer is yes, then overcoming your fear of public speaking will undoubtedly help you.

If you can manage to get over your anxiety of talking in front of a crowd, you have effectively just made yourself a bit braver in the process. You will find that since you are no longer afraid to share your thoughts to a group of people, you would also not have any problems asserting yourself and stop people from treating you like a docrmat.

Career and Educational Advancement

It is crucial that you learn to speak in front of an audience if you ever want to get ahead in school and at work. Just image this, your professor is talking about a topic that will be on your next big examination, but you have a question that you need to ask. Will you let your fear of speaking in public hinder you from raising your hand and asking a question? It's not worth failing a subject just because you are afraid of looking stupid for asking a question (which is not true).

You Will Become a Better Communicator

How many times have people misunderstood what you were saying? Are you beyond being tired of being told to "speak up" whenever you are trying to tell them something, but you can only mutter your words? Most people have trouble communicating because they do not know how to behave in front of others, and most of the time they are totally afraid to make fools of themselves. You have a choice to either languish in silence or let your voice be heard with confident.

Attract People

What makes people attractive? Is it their well-groomed hair? Maybe it's their Olympian physiques. Of course being physically attractive can be helpful in gaining the adoration of the masses, but the real selling point of people is their confidence. Look at politicians for instance, not all of them could be considered as the perfect human beings, but their constituents adore most of them. It is mostly because they have an outstanding presence, especially when they are delivering speeches.

If you can talk to people with the same kind of intensity and electrifying energy like most famous personalities, you will find that many people would want to listen and follow you, even if they have no idea of what message you're trying to convey.

Chapter 11: Find Your Niche

You want to be Top Dog in Public Speaking, right? **"Look, if you don't want to be the best, toss this book in the fireplace and take up basket weaving."**

You need to understand, to become the best public speaker you must be passionate about your public speaking career. You MUST, eat drink and sleep public speaking. You must be focused, determined and control any and all distractions to become successful in this field. It is an absolute must that you love what you're doing. Yes, it's important that you must enjoy helping people and be around people - communication is a two way process. **"The reason I do this basically is that I**

You need to know that in the public speaking world; if your subject is not what the public wants to hear, you're out of business. The more passion you exude about your topic, the more your audience will want to hear about it. So finding your particular niche is critical. So we need to search your gray matter to find out what your niche is. **Your audience will know if**

you're faking it! believe me! So, find your niche!

Ask yourself these questions; what do you like to do in your spare time? What are your hobbies? What do you like to do on holidays? What is your favorite travel destination?

What do you like to talk about with friends? What issue do you hold a strong opinion? What are you passionate about? What values do you stand for? What particular skills do you have? What special professional or personal experiences have you had in your life? Write these things down.

Now associate them. Let's say you like to talk about Donald Trump. Now write down all things that come up in your mind. All the things related to Donald Trump; example: real estate, business successes, scandals, TV productions, his friends, billionaire and so on. In other words, you are building a topic tree around Mr.

Trump. This process takes some time, but you can apply it on almost every issue.

Now you must use a trial and error process to determine if this is your niche. To do this take the example above and ask yourself the following questions. Is it of great interest to you? Does it really excite you? Is it something you're already interested in?

Did you always want to know more about it, but didn't have the time to find out? Do you love to talk about it? Are you passionate about your subject? Most importantly, regardless of the subject, YOU MUST BE PASSIONATE ABOUT PUBLIC SPEAKING AND THE TOPIC BE PRESENTED! You may perform this process several times in determining your niche. Don't get discouraged if you don't find it right away. You may think you have found it and later find out it really doesn't excite you or there is no market for that subject. If that is the case go through process again. You will find your niche! Don't stop with just one subject, as you are limiting yourself in the market. Determine if your niche can be broken into several and expand on them.

Once you have found your niche(s), perfect it/them. If you've noticed, you can have more than one. **Don't limit your marketability by settling on only one subject**. It is strongly suggested you offer several subjects. Personally, I have eleven seminars from one hour to a two week on site venue. Versatility is the name of the game. But which ever you choose, become the expert in that/those subject(s). Stay up to date with changes, technology or whatever impacts change to your subject. Constant research is the key here. Remember, people are paying for your knowledge!

Chapter 12: Overcoming The Anxiety

For the past few chapters, we've been talking about how detrimental the fear of speaking in front of a crowd could be. Such difficulties can cause you a business deal, your job or the opportunity to have it as well as valuable connections that could have moved you forward.

We have also established that these jitters are normal but it should not become a limiting factor since speaking or communicating is a very important skill that everyone needs in order to not only survive but thrive in life.

However, mastering it can open doors of opportunity for you one after the other. Having an exceptional amount of confidence, which you can acquire through public speaking, can help you differentiate yourself from the rest. Individuals who can communicate well have the power to influence and make a considerable impact on the lives of others. Furthermore, confidence in your skills and abilities can help you become more certain of yourself thus allowing you to project a strong and healthy image. With all these perks of mastering public speaking, why are a lot of people still entangled with social anxiety?

Here are a couple of things that you should remember to make the cut above the rest when it comes to overcoming shyness and social anxiety. Always remember that these conditions are normal but self-inflicted – you alone hold the key to liberate yourself.

1. Know what you're afraid of – over thinking is also a common practice when we have no idea of what to expect. More often than not, these thoughts and scenarios that we create in our heads are baseless and exaggerated. Checking things on the basis of facts and actual

probabilities can save you from a lot of stress. It is always good to be one step ahead to avoid getting caught off guard. Panicking out of fear before anything happens can only waste your time and energy.

2. Breathe – this simple technique is one of the most powerful methods to lessen social anxiety. Proper oxygen flow all over the body helps the brain to stay clear and focused in stressful situations such as speaking in front of an audience. Both clarity and focus are vital to keep yourself calm in such instances. Taking a couple of deep breaths can slow down your heart rate and calm your nerves as well.

3. Focus on yourself – delivering a speech or a statement is all about you. Since more often than not you present your own points of view, minding how people react or what they're thinking during your time at the podium is irrelevant. Remember to only compete with yourself to ensure your

growth as a public speaker. Looking at others for affirmation is a good practice to keep yourself humble and abreast with best practices that others might be applying. Just be weary of over doing it because it has been proven to be detrimental.

4. Relax – just like breathing, you would have to consciously make an effort to calm yourself when delivering a speech. This is most especially needed before and during presentations since these parts are more nerve-wrecking. Use positive self talk and scenario building to keep everything as calm as water. Breathing may also be integrated with these thoughts for better results

5. Practice – practicing doesn't make anything perfect because nothing will ever be. However, simulations or rehearsals in front of the mirror or family members can help you eliminate errors during the actual presentation. Being able to correct

yourself as well as getting to improve your speech beforehand is a rare chance that shouldn't be taken for granted.

In the next chapter, we should take a look on how to best prepare for a public speaking engagement.

Nothing Beats Preparedness

Feelings of fear or panic that may take over an individual when called to give a speech performance in front of a crowd is said to be caused by a number of factors. One of the most common ones is shyness which affects people of all ages, backgrounds and cultures around the globe. Handling it may also vary from one person to another. People who are more proactive may use this feeling to challenge themselves and apply it to new goals. Others, especially the younger ones, may opt to go with the flow by hiding in their shells which is not at all that beneficial to anyone.

You can never be too prepared for a speaking engagement. Since public speaking is the art of conversing with a group of people in a structured and deliberate manner, preparation is a key component of this task. Ample time to organize and practice one's speech is usually given to pre-arranged events such as conventions, meetings, weddings or other formal gatherings. But being asked to speak impromptu in an event is unavoidable. Moreover, it should not be a reason to strain your image or dampen a joyful event.

To avoid reaping the negative effects of social anxiety, here are some tips on how to prepare well for a presentation or a speaking engagement in just a few steps.

▪ **Knowing the event** is a primary thing that a speaker should do once invited to grace a gathering. Being able to know the purpose and reason of an event will guide through further decisions that you'll have to make all through out the preparation period. Familiarizing oneself with these can also help in giving impromptu speeches since it allows one to set in the proper direction.

- Many people fear speaking in front of a crowd because of the audience. Horror stories on nasty and ruthless audiences have been witnessed and passed on from one speaker to another. But **studying your audience** can do you much good in this department. Getting a clear picture of who or what kind of people your audience are can be your guide not only in determining appropriate words to use but also the speaking style to use as well.

- Select the theme of your thoughts to keep your speech together. Cramping your speech with several little ideas from various topics isn't going to help your audience appreciate it. Remember that your key goal is to send your message across correctly.

- After setting things straight, you may now **highlight your key point** or the most important message that your speech contains. Generally, you would want this to be the only message that your audience retain if ever they happen to forget everything else.
- **Craft the perfect form** of your speech by organizing its structure. Make sure that the topics you talk about are arranged in a logical manner. Usually, deductive and inductive techniques are used for structuring purposes.
- No one wants a boring speaker and his speech! **Add colour to your shape** or structured speech by using humour, anecdotes or wit to tint your speeches.
- **Do it all over again** – double or maybe even triple check your speech for grammatical errors and possible inconsistencies. Doing so may also help you improve its content. Another purpose of checking is to see which parts are in

need of external boost like emphasis, props or the use of queue cards to ensure that you don't miss anything important.

Chapter 13: Yourself

The only person in the world that you can control is you.

Sometimes having self-control is easier said than done. In order for this to happen, you need to believe that you can do it.

The best way to believe that something can happen is to have small success to build up your confidence. You know what you want to say so we are going to do 3 things:

Practice (on film and/or in the mirror)

Practice (one on one with friend)

Practice (with a small group)

It is not enough to just to practice, we have to practice as though it is the real thing.

Let's start with your body.

Body

Your body and your voice are the tools that you will need to master in order to persuade your audience to believe you. You should have good posture because this projects confidence to you and your audience. The quality of your voice is also a whole lot better when you maintain proper posture while delivering your speech. Notice the posture of great speakers, their body language is positive.

Notice the welcoming openness of the image to the right.

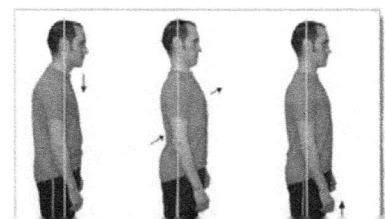

Notice the slouch, the overextended chest and the correct posture.

The 2-minute Power Pose

When your body is in a positive state for two minutes, you actually start to feel more confident.

According to a study at Harvard, your testosterone level (confidence) will go up and your cortisone level (stress) will go down. This applies to men and women.

Here is an exact quote:

"In both human and non-human primates, expansive, open postures reflect high power, whereas contractive, closed postures reflect low power (Carney, Hall, & Smith LeBeau, 2005; Darwin, 1872/2009; de Waal, 1998; Hall, Coats, & Smith LeBeau, 2005). Not only do these postures reflect power, they also produce it; in contrast to adopting low power poses, adopting high power poses increases explicit and implicit feelings of power and dominance, risk-taking behavior, action orientation, pain tolerance, and testosterone (the dominance hormone), while reducing stress, anxiety, and cortisol (the stress hormone; Bohns & Wiltermuth, 2011; Carney, Cuddy, & Yap, 2010; Carney, Yap, Lucas, Mehta, Ferrero, McGee, & Wilmuth, under review; Huang, Galinsky, Gruenfeld, & Guillory, 2011). Moreover, compared to classic power manipulations that do not involve nonverbal behavior, such as role assignments and power recall primes, adopting high-power poses leads to stronger effects on thought abstraction and action orientation (Huang et al., 2011). "

Example of High Power & Low Power Poses:

Remember to power up just before you go on stage. Your body will maintain a lot of that power as you go about in delivering your message.

Voice

Once you have your body in a positive state, you can now concentrate on your voice. You should articulate your words in a way that is more pronounced than normal. I don't mean to be "over-the-top" but if you pronounce them a little more concise, you will hear the difference. This will give your words impact and power.

Also, you will want to act out the words with your voice. For example, if you say that you were excited about something within your message, make the tone of your voice have excitement. If you're talking about a sad part, make the tone match it.

Giving a dazzling message is about having a strong message that connects with your audience. It is about taking the listener on an emotional journey. You take them on this journey by acting out or feeling the words that you are saying. If the message is something that you are passionate about, it will come naturally.

Pauses in your speech can help you give emphasis to a major point. For example, I might say: "As I was researching the problem, I discovered an interesting fact." (PAUSE) Next, state the fact that you discovered. (PAUSE BRIEFLY AGAIN) Now tell them why it was such an important discovery. Make your case solid. In this scenario, you have the audience wondering **what this interesting fact is**. By taking that pause, you have effectively intensified their curiosity.

Sometimes before you go out to deliver your message, your voice may tighten up. There's a simple little exercise that you can do to have your voice go to its natural condition.

Hummmm.

Humming lowers your voice to its natural pitch, because your voice tends to be higher if you are overly excited or nervous.

Chapter 14: Body Of The Speech: Get To The Point And Stay Focused

"If you have an important point to make, don't try to be subtle or clever. Use a pile driver. Hit the point once. Then come back and hit it again. Then hit it a third time a tremendous whack."

— Winston S. Churchill.
The structure of the speech comprise of three parts:

☐ Introduction telling audience what you are going to tell them;

☐ Body of the speech – telling the audience the main points.

☐ Conclusion highlighting and summarizing the main points again.

The body of the speech is the biggest part of any speech. It is where the majority of information is communicated and the central theme is explained and emphasized. It requires careful presentation of ideas, substantiation and effective organization of thoughts. The speech should be organized in a manner that all the information and ideas, culminates and reinforce the core message of your speech. The information should run through the body of your speech unifying them together. The best "organizers" act as a mechanism for the audience to grasp and remember what you say. A good body of speech is specific and gives vivid and clear ideas that persuasively support your main point.

Effective body of the speech: Some measures

1. Pain – Struggle – Overcoming – Learning (PSOL): The main body must comprise of certain problem or pain which poses the challenge. Then there has to the description of the struggle which should end with overcoming or winning the over struggle or challenge. Finally, there should be learnings or take away message for the audience on the basis of lesson learnt by the speaker or the character of the story or example. If the speech is technical in nature, the pattern could be Problem - Cause – Solution. The pattern of citing the problems, causes of the problems and the solution is the appropriate one.

2. Organization Ideas: Once the broad structure of the body of the speech is determined it is important to organize your ideas in a manner that audience could follow it easily. Since it is the biggest part of your speech, organizing is critical. There are various ways of organizing a speech. You can use it as per your comfort level or the topic.

a) Acronyms: Acronyms are an excellent way to organize your speech. It enables the individual letters representing a keyword summarizing each sub-point. It also works as an tool for remembering the key points both by the speaker and the audience. For instance, if your speech is about leadership you can use the acronym LEADER representing L- Love for people, E- Ethical, A– Attitude, D- Daring, E – Energetic and R- Relentless.

b) Issues: Speech can also be organized on the basis of different dimensions for instance 'physical- psychologicalspiritual' aspects or 'personal-socialpolitical' issues or 'economic growth vs inequality' or 'rationality vs faith' or 'science and arts' etc. Depending on the topics, such segregation helps better organization of ideas.

c) Opinions: Speech can also be organized into opinions given by various experts, scientist or school of thoughts. Organization of speech on different view points is effective especially for technical and research oriented topics. What is a classical school of thought, current research and future issues provide logical structure for the body of the speech.

d) Storylines: Use of stories are very suitable for demarking the distinct points in your speech.

e) Time: The progression of events or research in the past, present and future is the most easily understood structure that can be followed for an effective organization of speech.

3. Focus on a core message:
The core message should be the anchor of

your speech. This would enable the speaker to remain focused and to keep audience's attention fixed on the central theme. Sprinkling the ideas without any core message or linking it to core message makes the body of speech ineffective.

4.   Rules   of   three: A speech should have not more than three main key points or examples substantiating the core message. Anything more than that makes it difficult for the audience to grasp. When there are three points or examples, it is far easier for the audience to remember your ideas and their inter-linkages. Anything more dilutes the focus. You can use a story or statistics/facts or personal experience to substantiate your central theme. However, it is better to use the combination of these three elements as it will appeal to a larger audience. Hence, choose your topic and support the same with three points. Each paragraph containing a story, facts or statistic and a human experience.

5. Relate and link ideas together: The body of speech is the biggest part of speech. We tend to describe the problem and struggle around it. Then we describe how the speaker or the character in the story or technology has overcome the problem. Finally, what are the key take away or the lessons learnt which has relevance for the audience. All the ideas, anecdote and statistics should be synchronized to thrust the core message of the speech. Hence, it is essential to clearly show the interconnections between various ideas and examples.

6. Proper transitions: Transitions are important in all types of communication. They're even more so in public speaking than in writing or even interpersonal communication. Since in public speaking one cannot revert back or ask for repetition as it impairs the flow.

However, the transitions are often overlooked by the speaker. Consequently, despite a good content, they fail to put across their ideas to the audience. Most often, speakers fumble in transitions. Hence, what is important is smooth transitions, which is the mark of the professional public speaker. It is just like moving from one gear to another while driving a car. This will enable the audience to follow the speech and grasp the message in an easy manner. The transition is like guidepost which enables the audience to know that there is a change or shift from one phase one to another. Transition enables the audience to gauge the direction and progress in the speech and relationships between the major ideas.

Tools of Transitions:

There are many transition style, which can be used depending on the comfort of the speaker, the theme of the speech and the audience.

a) Point-by-point transition: The easiest transition is when the ideas are spelt out in points. When we speak and state ideas into one, two, three, four etc. It is very easy to capture the ideas and makes transitions smooth. When we mention a statement or idea and say that there are three important reasons to substantiate it. The audience immediately gets attuned to listen to those three reasons and moves from being general into the specific.

b) Question: A question can serve as a good transition. It can be very effective in shifting the audience's attention. For instance, if you are speaking on leadership, you can use this question for transition, "Now that we have seen the importance of a leader, can we now discuss what the essential characteristics of a leader are?" This question summarizes what has been discussed and leads to the subsequent sub point. One can also move to the next point by asking a question like "Would you now like to know what makes a leader effective?" Or "Do you know that leaders are made, not born?".

c) Physical movement: Movement from one part of the stage to another can also be used to show transition from one part of the speech to another. Movement from left, centre and right could be used for representing the transition from the past, present and future. One can use a movement from back and front to indicate progress from one point to another. Movement of hands, breathing patterns and shrinking of the body could also be used to present one's idea more forcefully.

d) Stories: Stories are an excellent way of making a point and also transition to another point. The method of 'tell a story make a point' works excellent in creating smooth transitions.

Transitions enable the audience to follow the speech. It gives them requisite break and generates renewed attention. Mastering transitions segregate your speech into manageable chunks. It helps in distinctly highlighting different subunits within the speech. As a result, the audience is quite aware of what stage of speech they are in and what is next to come. Transitions work as milestone or lighthouse to enable the audience to follow and absorb your ideas. Smooth transitions give the speaker and the audience the sense of control on what is going on. It also makes audience understand speech in a better manner.

7. Display good command over topic: You cannot speak well if you do not know your subject. The body of the speech is not to get attention, which is done during the opening of the speech. A speaker has to convince the audience his point of view by displaying his command over the topic with various examples, anecdote and facts. The credibility of the speaker is formed in the body of the speech, which is the actual field to win over the audience with his communication skills.

8. Talk in picture: Kindle the imagination it will forge the connection with the audience. Instead of saying, "In the battlefield, 21 soldiers were killed with the bullets as soon as they encountered the enemy. The US Army head was jolted. He changed the strategy and decided to strike by Air rather than Infantry. It was a fierce battle which resulted in heavy casualty of the enemy country."

Give more vivid description, "In the battlefield, as soon as they encountered the enemy, the shower of sharp long bullets pierced the chest of 7 soldiers and red thick blood started oozing out their broad masculine chest like hot red lava and soon the soil bathed with blood and bodies. The US Army head was red in anger and shocked at the same time. He changed the strategy and decided to strike by Air rather than Infantry. It was a fierce battle which resulted in heavy casualty of the enemy country and hill town of Afghanistan literally turned into the crematory ground."

9. Power punch statement:
As a speaker, it is important to think of some tagline statement in your speech. People are not going to remember your speech. However, they would remember power punch statements in your speech. Such statement catches their imagination. For instance,

"A government that is of the people, by the people, for the people, shall not perish from the earth." (Abraham Lincoln, "The Gettysburg Address", November 19, 1863)

"blood, sweat and tears," Winston Churchill, ("Blood,

Sweat, and Tears" May 13, 1940, London), "Give me blood, and I will give you freedom" (Netaji Subhash Chandra Bose, 1944)

"Duty, Honor, Country" (General Douglas MacArthur, "Duty, Honor, Country", May 12, 1962),

The body of the speech is critical as it is here that you use all your public speaking skills to win over the audience. It is the main field, where you have to convince your audience. Howsoever, impressive your opening of speech may be, it will have no effect if the content and delivery in the body is poor or weak.

Chapter 15: **Become A 'Perfect Presenter'**
- Introduction
- Vocal techniques
  - Tone, pitch, projection and inflection
- Harnessing body language
  - Employing an open stance
  - Maintaining eye contact

- Maintaining eye contact
  o Why eye contact is important
  o How to maintain eye contact with a large audience
- Dress to impress
  o Knowing how to dress for your audience
- Section Review

Up to this point we have built your presentation skills and given you some techniques to ensure that you are ready and able to give a great presentation. In this section we will take it one step further and build on the skills you have learnt to give you some ways to truly impress your audience.

Vocal Techniques

Do you know what you sound like when you talk? I remember being somewhat shocked when, as a child, I first recorded my voice on a cassette recorder and played it back. We often sound very different from what we hear ourselves. I suggest that you take a presentation or a passage from a book and read it aloud while recording yourself.

Now, what did you hear? And, more importantly, did what you heard sound like someone you would like to listen to for a period of time? By this I mean, did you sound interesting and passionate about what you said or was it more monotone?

Of course, this is not a fair test, but you need to consider how you speak. Verbal communication is vital to any presenter; not only is it essential for you to get your message across, but it can also impart trust and confidence to your audience.

Harnessing Body Language

You have probably heard of the phrase 'body language', and in fact you will be using it subliminally all the time. Body language is the set of non-verbal messages we send; in fact, research says that 80% of our communication is nonverbal and that over 50% is from body language.

Body language portrays how we really feel. A good example is when you are having an argument with someone – if you were to watch their body language you may find that they have their arms crossed, effectively blocking you out.

Using body language as a presenter can be very powerful, particularly using an open stance. This is when you use body language to be open to your audience and take down any barriers. To use an open stance:

- look at how you hold your body – you will likely to be standing when you present, however if you are not, uncross your legs.
- open your arms – use open, slow gestures with your arms, incorporating embracing movements with your palms relaxed towards the audience (don't rapidly wave your fist at the audience, for example.)

- maintain eye contact with your audience – I'll tell you more on the next page!

Body language comes from human beings' very earliest days on the planet, and the open stance works at a very low level in the brain, showing that you are not going to attack the other person and in fact that you are holding yourself open to them.

You should also watch your audience's body language – overall are they responding with open body language or are there many crossed arms showing resistance to you? Are people maintaining your eye contact? In particular look for head nodding, showing direct agreement and subliminally providing positive feedback for you as presenter.

Maintaining Eye Contact

An important part of your body language is maintaining eye contact, you can see this when you are talking with someone one to one. You can very quickly tell if someone is not telling the truth or if they are bored when they do not keep eye contact with you. You can send the same message as a presenter if you do not maintain eye contact with your audience.

Now, of course, if you have a large audience you cannot attempt to look directly at everyone, but you can give the impression that you are. The trick is to select two or three people who are distributed in your audience – for example, if it is a theatre style environment, one or two people on the left hand side and one or two on the right – then, as you speak, look towards these people and try to maintain eye contact, changing the people you look at regularly but not too often. It is good to perhaps glance up from your cue cards and change person or to do so when you change slide.

By doing this there will be groups of the audience who will believe that you are making eye contact with them.

Dress to impress

Part of being a Power Presenter is being in control of your entire environment, this means not just how you are presenting your content, but also how you are presenting yourself.

Before you present you need to be aware of how you should dress. Unfortunately, the days of business dress being a suit and tie for gentlemen and business attire for ladies is now changing, many organisations now have smart causal rules and you can run the risk of turning up and being over- or underdressed for your presentation.

There is an important consideration however, and that is, how would you usually dress for this presentation? The most important thing to remember is that you should be comfortable in your clothes. This is not just in the way they fit, but also how they make you feel. We are trying to build your own confidence and then pass this to the audience, so find clothes that make you feel empowered. Of course you should not turn up in something totally unsuitable (unless that is the impact you wish to make – be careful!) but something that makes you feel right.

They say that clothes maketh the man (or woman!), but it is the confidence with which you wear them that goes much further.

Section Review

In this section we have started to use techniques to develop your presence, voice and body language with your audience. We have:

• understood the importance of good vocal technique

• learnt about body language both as a presenter and how to read your audience

• learnt the importance of eye contact and how to maintain eye contact with a large audience

• understood how to dress as a presenter.

Now we will go on to use storytelling to create a believable and interesting presentation.

Using Storytelling For Presentations
- Introduction
- Why use stories?
- A Poor Presentation
- What lets presentations down
- The Narrative Arc
  - Introduction to the Narrative Arc
  - Presentations as stories
  - Understanding the Narrative Arc
  - The elements of the arc
- Creating a story for your presentation
- Using the Narrative Arc
- Questions to be answered when using the arc
- The Presentation Storyboard
  - Using a storyboard template for your presentations
  - Shoot the bullets
  - Adding impact with images
- Section Review

What was the last film you saw? Even if it wasn't all that good, I am sure you could describe the story and tell me the ending. In fact you could probably remember a lot of detail about the whole story.

It's likely that the story involved you and maybe even made you feel happy or sad. No doubt you empathised with the hero and were on the edge of your seat when it looked like the baddies might actually win!

Now, think back to the last presentation you saw – did you feel any emotion? Or were you just dying to get out of the room? Do you remember the ending or any of the detail of the presentation itself? The answer is, unfortunately, probably not.

But why is that?

A poor presentation

If the above slide looks familiar, it is not a surprise that many presentations are unmemorable. However, it is not just the busy text and the poor design that lets this one down. For a presentation to be memorable you need to engage the audience – basically, you need to tell them a story.

The Narrative Arc

The telling of stories goes back many centuries; in fact, it is an ancient tradition which covers everything from cave paintings to Bridget Jones' Diary. We are very familiar with the ways that stories are told and often we come to expect a certain pattern and delivery; this is called the narrative arc: **Understanding the Narrative Arc**

You should remember when you give a presentation that, just like a story, there should be a clear beginning, middle and end. The Narrative Arc graph may look a little complicated, however the concept is quite simple. The line on the graph shows how we should be bringing the audience from a state where they (effectively) know nothing, through a stage of confrontation where we have to face a number of issues, to a place where their knowledge is higher and there is a clear resolution.

For example, if we split a simple story into the narrative arc:

- Set The Scene Face
- The Issues
- Come To A Resolution
- Meet three pigs
- Pigs build inadequate houses
- Stone House
- Meet wolf (protagonist)
- Wolf starts to blow them down
- Wolf Fricassee

We set the scene, creating a shared introduction before the confrontation, in this case the wolf wanting to eat the pigs before we reach the resolution, happy pigs, unhappy wolf.

You may question how you might use this method with a presentation? Well, we should still have the same steps. For example: **Set The Scene**

- Identify the reason for needing a new IT system **Face The Issues**
- Getting buy-in from all departments Come To A Resolution
- Improved customer service Using the Narrative Arc

Let's be truthful here, we are not expecting you to create a Hollywood blockbuster out of your next presentation, but by using the narrative tools you create something that will be more intuitive to your audience.

To create the narrative arc for a presentation you need to look at the content and ask some questions:

- Why am I here? – This is not the meaning of life, but at least the meaning of the presentation! What do people expect to have achieved by the end of the presentation. This may be certain knowledge, a decision or a call to action.
- Where do I start? – What is the common ground from which you need to start? It is

good to start with a question, (for example — why are we not delivering great customer service? Why is our IT system failing?) This should be a common question which your pre-presentation research shows the audience will want to be answered.

● Where do we want to be? — What is the expected resolution?

This should be the outcome for the presentation.

● What are the issues? — What is stopping us reaching the resolution? These are the barriers which we need to overcome and the issues that we need to face.

With this information you should be able to create a presentation storyboard.

Presentation Storyboard

We need to use the narrative arc to create a simple storyboard for your presentation. The storyboard will allow you not only to ensure you cover all of the stages of the arc, but will also allow you to create accurate timings for your presentation.

Shoot the bullets

The other technique you should look at when creating your presentation from the storyboard is to avoid bullet points. Remember:

- the screen is not your script – you have cue cards.

- we don't want to just list the content on the screen for the audience to read.

If you do, just ignore the presentation and send them an email.

- a picture says a thousand words.

Instead of pages of bullets (remember the poor presentation from earlier in this section) which the audience will read or just ignore, use photographs, graphics or images. You can find great photos on the internet from sites such as Pixabay www.pixabay.com which provides many free or cost-effective photos you can use.

Put a photo up on a full screen and do the talking yourself rather than the bullet points. The image should be used to add impact!

Section Review

In this section we reviewed how to use storytelling to create a powerful presentation. We:

- understood why storytelling is important
- learnt about the narrative arc and how to use it for presentations
- gave our presentation a beginning, middle and end
- created a storyboard to build our presentation
- got rid of bullet points to add impact without words.

In the next section you will learn how to deal with anything that could possibly go wrong during your presentation and how to deal with it!

Chapter 16: How To Be Confident On Stage

When you are finally delivering your speech, but are still encountering fear and nervousness, what do you do? This chapter will help you with your problem. In this chapter, you will find some tips and techniques on how to overcome fear while delivering your speech in public.

Introduction plays a big part in your speech delivery. It gives your audience a hint on what your speech is all about, and it gives them an impression of how you will be delivering it. A lousy introduction may lead them to conclude that you have a weak and unplanned presentation, thus they will be less interested to listen. It is important to start strong in your introductory speech. If you need to shout, do it. It will not only release your fear, it will also encourage attention.

While delivering your speech, it is important to maintain engagement with your audience, but that does not mean that you look at them at all times. Look at your audience, but do not look at a particular one. Establish connection, but do not let it distract you. Too much engagement and eye contact with the audience may lead you to become more conscious. Just imagine that you are talking to nobody, and do as you practice. Keep in mind the things that you have noted while you were recording or practicing your speech.

The next thing to remember is never apologize. You can only do this if you happen to mention wrong information, but as much as possible, avoid saying sorry. If you stutter or if you forget your lines, then just go on with your speech. Apologizing would mean lack of preparation and inadequate knowledge of your topic. Do not mind the reaction of the audience. Your mistakes will become more obvious if you apologize. Just continue delivering your speech, without letting the responses of the people watching distract you.

It is important to remind yourself to speak at a moderate pace. When you are nervous, the tendency is for you to speak very fast. This will increase the possibility that you will stutter and forget your lines, or worse, your audience will not understand what you are saying. There will be a greater tendency that you will only eat the words that you are saying, making your speech difficult to understand. Even if you are nervous, try to speak at a normal pace so that your audience will understand you.

Lastly, do not be very serious in your speech. If you condition your speech to be a serious one, you will tend to become more nervous and afraid. It would not hurt if you try to add humor in your speech and make the mood light. Not only will it help you overcome fear in public speaking, it will also be enjoyable for your audience.

Now that you know some of the basic reminders and tips that will help you overcome your fear while you are delivering your speech on stage, it will be important to hear from the world's greatest and most famous public speakers. Their experiences will be helpful in your journey to becoming an effective public speaker. In the next chapter, you will learn of some of the tips and advice of the greatest speakers of time. You can use this to improve yourself and to make your speech a lot more effective.

Chapter 17: How To Seat Your Audience

Go For Comfort and Moderation
In any public gathering comfort should be your number one priority. If your participants are not comfortable chances are they will get bored in the middle of your presentation and loss interests. That is not healthy for your speaking business.

Furthermore, they must not be too comfortable to the extent they'll fall asleep in the middle of your presentation. In anything you do, moderation should be your watch word. The Bible says, **"Let your moderation be known unto all men"** (Philippians 4:5).

Secondly, be sure the chairs are well seated, well arranged and of equal level so everyone can have a perfect view.

And finally, there should be space enough to give room for free and easy movement without anyone disturbing anyone. And you should also have spare chairs that can be easily reach or move around for late comers or for any one who feels will need additional chair to get the best from your presentation.

Another issue to consider is to give room for question and answer at the end of your presentation. This will encourage your audience to ask questions related to your presentation in order to be clarify from doubts or uncertain issues.

Allowing room for questions will encourage responses from different quarters from your audience. You will know how far you have gone.

Chapter 18: Methods Of Communication In Public Speaking

The traditional techniques used to communicate in public speaking usually rely on oratory and an audience. But advances in technology have brought about more sophisticated means of communication, which have revolutionised the way public speakers communicate with their audience. For instance, long distance communications technologies such as audience response systems, using smartphones and laptops and video-conferencing, are becoming increasingly popular in use across the world.

Video-conferencing is designed to serve a conference or multiple locations, reducing the need for people to travel. It brings people together by enabling multiple locations to communicate by simultaneous two-way-video and audio transmissions. Video-conferencing technologies also enable speakers to share documents with their aucience and allow the display of information on whiteboards.

Benefits that flow from Overcoming Fear of Public Speaking

There are other notable benefits that can flow from learning to overcome the fear of speaking in public, that are often overlooked. One can benefit from it personally, in the improvement of one's character and personality. Here are some of the most significant benefits that you can reap.

Builds Self-Confidence

Overcoming fear of public speaking can help to build a person's self-confidence. And a person who is self-assured is usually more out-going and sociable. Their attitude and outlook on life tend to be positive, making way for a more fulfilled life. Instead of allowing their fears to get the better of them, they usually find ways to tackle life's challenges and adversities in order to achieve the outcome they desire.

Builds Self-Esteem

Developing your self-esteem is another benefit that can be achieved from overcoming the fear of speaking before the public. Self-esteem is a measure of how one values or regards one's self. A self-confident person usually has high self-esteem, whereas a person with low self-esteem lacks self-confidence. So, developing a high degree of self-esteem is a valuable social attribute, as it makes one feels confident about one's self. This is an important factor in helping a person to overcome the fear of speaking in public.

Improves Communication Skills

Being able to communicate well is an essential skill for social interaction, which is another benefit that can be developed from overcoming the fear of public speaking. Fear can affect a person's ability to communicate well, which can adversely affect how they interact with others. Having good communications skills will help to make a person feel more confident when speaking in public. A confident speaker will feel more comfortable when speaking in public and will therefore be unlikely to be distracted by feeling fearful. The speaker will be able to focus better on the topic for discussion and be able to interact well with an audience. Some speakers do get very apprehensive about question and answer sessions (Q&A), so this is a very valuable skill to develop.

Better Listening Skills

Active listening is an essential skill for effective communication. This is a skill that one can develop with practice. It is necessary, when communicating with your audience, to make a conscious effort to listen carefully so that you understand what is being said. This is necessary to interact well with your audience and to respond accordingly. You will develop active listening skills over time, leading to improved communication. Your audience will benefit too, as your active listening skills will allow more successful interaction.

Improves Voice Projection

A speaker who has difficulty with voice projection can benefit, as the successful delivery of a speech requires a speaker to speak clearly and pronounce words correctly. Proper voice projection can be achieved through formal training or through practising one's speech. A person who is able to project their voice with confidence will feel more comfortable in front of an audience. Being distracted by being fearful, which prevents a speaker from giving their full attention to the delivery of their speech, is then unlikely to happen.

Chapter 19: Why How To Make Money Speaking Is Unique

Wisdom and knowledge is granted unto thee; and I will **give thee riches**, and wealth, and honor, such as none of the kings have had that have been before thee, neither shall there any after thee have the like.

II Chronicles 1:12, **Emphasis Added**

Whom he called together with the workman of like occupation, and said, Sirs, ye know that **by this craft we have our wealth.**

Act 19: 25, Emphasis Added

The subject of money is a very sensitive one in all fields of human endeavors regardless of sex, race, color or nationality. **A lot has been said about money or the art of making money, whether ethically, legally or otherwise.**

But this book, **How 2 Make Money Speaking** which, from now on I will refer to as **H2MMS!** is quite different from any other book you've probably read on the art of making money.

And I really can't see any other book I can recommend to you that unveils **the most astonishing secret to making money,** depending on your financial target based primarily on your own gift, talent, ability . . . or words – by just speaking on what you know, have, or love talking about than this.

Most books about the arts of making money with your natural gift, talent, or ability would promise you Heaven and Earth only to offer you puffy clouds or **help you cultivate frustration** at the end of the day.

Tragically, many of them are just repetition of what you've already known, and even better than the writers themselves, only to **get you bored with their endless hypes and gimmicks!**

Unfortunately, most of them don't even offer **practical ways or advice on how to go about turning words into money,** thus, herein lies the biggest problem and failure of all these get-rich-quick writers with their bogus claim, both online and offline.

Friend, believe me. I have spent a huge sum of money looking for a simple and yet, most practical ways to make money with just what I love doing whatever that doing is, with little or no capital involved and I have found none! Not until recently when **I was hit by a miraculous stone.**

And I believe you don't want to loss money as much as I've lost before you discovered that all your life you've been living inside the very secret to making money without knowing. If that is the case, then your story is not different from a fool who walks through the forest and sees no firewood.

Well, who wants to lose money after all?

Just recently I was surfing the Net when I came across a book title with the sub-titled, **"The Best Revenge is to Make Big Money".** Wow! And that is what H2MMS! offers with your natural ability – **revenge against every of your financial failures and limitations.**

The Honey and the Vinegar

OK. Remember our honey versus vinegar scenario? Yup!

A Painful Revelation

Alright, imagine one of these network companies giving you 3GB every week for a year to access the Internet.

Let's assume they offer you freebie gigabytes (gb) because they know your mindset and understand what you want – to access the Internet and brows some of these social networking sites, chat with your friends, check your email, make research, do other online business (if you're an infoPreneur) and so on.

Now, if care is not taken you would probably patronize the company for a lifetime (as their customer) and even invite your household and friends to follow your lead, ordering for their services and paying a higher rate than necessary (without knowing since in every company's law the word, **Terms and Conditions Applied**).

Right? Very well!

Ok. Imagine another scenario. An MD or CEO of a successful company patronizing the same networking company; buys and order some of their services like you did but in a larger quantity.

Now do you think the same company would offer the same freebies they offered you in the first scenario? I doubt! It would be something higher than that! Why? Because the MD or CEO is a potential customer! He (or she) demands and order their services and pay huge sum of money for it!

Here they would probably offer him 500GB a month! Or maybe a winning car or lottery ticket to travel to Hawaii or Dubai for being a potential customer.

This is one of the real reasons rich people often get away with big prizes in a promo such as expensive cars, houses, and a trip to abroad (or Disneyland) and so on.

But how do they do it?

Is it because the companies are rich and have enough money to throw around? Maybe! Is it because they want you to believe they don't play gimmicks but rather keeps to their promises? Maybe! Or is it because they want to win new customers and retain the old ones? Maybe!

You see, all of these reasons are very true except for the first option. But this may come to you as a shock: where do you think they get all the money they throw around awarding some of their supposedly winners or faithful loyalists?

YOU!

Oh, you're surprise? Yes, you! You, you, you! You who consider yourself to be poor, miserable-church-rat and thus, believe in such arid nonsense!

They use your money to reward their potential customers! To add to the wealth and make members of their own clique richer than you!

They use your own money to give themselves or members of their clique that very comfort and luxury you've been denying yourself.

Oh, that sucks, doesn't it?!

And isn't what all these financial institutions do? Of course, they use your money in the bank by loaning it to the rich guys while the rich guys use your own money to enrich themselves, making them richer than yourself but with whose money? Yes, your guess is as good as mine if you're thinking what I'm thinking: you!

Alright, let me reveal another stunning secret. Every communication industry you pay allegiance to as their customer knows the exact airtime (credit or recharge card) you often load into your cell phone.

If you're fun of loading N100 airtime (since that's your economic power, for example, they know. Tragically, most of them don't even look at it that way. Every amount you load into your phone reflects in their data base; and the same goes with someone who loads N200, N500 or other higher version of airtime. And they are all segmented.

So those who loaded a higher version of airtime, say, N1,500 almost every day and spend almost half a million or more a month in recharging their phone have a higher likelihood of winning expensive gifts in a promo than the ones who spends N3,000 every two to three months recharging their phones.

Consequently, in terms of customer care and service, they respond promptly to the one who spend half a million or more a month buying their products and services than the one who spend just N3,000 for three months.

For the later, they just play arid music until his ears start bringing pulse before they attend to him!

Now, do you think every company will treat all of their customers the same? Hardly! And we both know it. Some customers are given a first hand or preferential treatment than others even though . . .

1 Both of them are their customers.

2 Both of them buy the same products.

3 Both of them patronize the same company.

4 But the way and manner the company looks at the two customers are different!

Now, if you're an intelligent reader you should know and understand what I'm

talking about. To be successful in your speaking business you must know and understand some of the techniques to use to appeal, attract, promise and like honey, catch different people who have shown interest in your service, product or information even if you want to talk about how to prepare the local African salad!

Consequently, try to **use the right words for the right individual.** For example, if you use the right headlines like, **"How to Prepare Delicious African Salad",** you would be successful if it is directed to Africans, or to Africans-Americans than to the Europeans.

If you study the history of successful speakers who have built successful business around their speaking events, you would see the reasons why they became successful after all. And it's wise to follow their footsteps.

They have used some of the approaches explained in this book to achieve the same level of success that you probably hope to reach in yours.

So I'll tell you this: You can build a successful speaking business around what you know – and offer it as a service, product or information.

Chapter 20: My (Bad) Experience With Public Speaking

I remember as a junior in a well-populated high school in Texas when I had to present in front of my science class. The teacher asked us students to create an invention, illustrate it on paper, color it, and present it to the class. I thought deeply to myself, focused on creating not something I wanted, **but something I could present without making a fool out of myself**. That was my main concern. I didn't want to be laughed at and give students a reason to bug me the rest of the school year. I believe all this thinking only made the ordeal worse, because this day turned out to be one of the worst days of my life.

On this day, I sat in class, rolling the pencil between my two hands. I could feel my hands starting to sweat as I looked up at the clock ticking continuously, with each tick advising me that I had less and less time to finish my assignment. I couldn't focus; and my body began to feel worse. I began to feel a sharp pain in my chest that lasted one or two seconds; that pain that's a manifestation of severe anxiety. I also started taking deep breaths more often, trying to calm myself down. I was too focused on how to present and survive scrutiny by about thirty students that I lost track of time.

My stomach ached when my teacher stood up, picked up his sleeves, and yelled, "Five minutes left, class." I was in deep. I had not started the assignment. I was an intelligent kid, but the fear of public speaking crippled me intellectually.

As a last-minute effort to avoid being the only student who didn't complete the assignment, and likely shamed in front of class for it, I drew a robot. A robot might not seem like a wonderful invention, but mine was, or so I thought. My robot had the ability to make sandwiches and churn them out through its abdomen. I rushed, trying to finish my assignment before the first student presented. Even more so, I rushed because I could have been the first student to present.

Luckily, I wasn't chosen to be the first sheep fed to the wolves. (This analogy conveys how much I hated public speaking). A classmate, young, short, and fragile was chosen. She presented eloquently, nonetheless, and described her invention persuasively—in fact, I think I would have purchased it if it was up for sale. The object she drew was a pink camera, with a wide, circular lens. The camera seemed not to be anything special, but then she explained why it was. "This camera," she said, "has the ability to enlarge an image one thousand times. It is equipped with normal and microscopic lenses. The microscopic lens allows us to zoom in on objects we can't see with the naked eye and take pictures of those objects to then transfer them to our personal computers." Through dialogue, she had turned something ordinary into something extraordinary. The power of speech, I thought.

As I sat there thinking how creative she was and how cool it'd be to possess such a camera, I also started thinking how high she had set the bar. Sometimes we do things other people perceive as terrible in themselves; sometimes we do things other people perceive as terrible **compared to other things**. My presentation, I thought, would be an instance of the latter. Here was this bright girl, with some degree of confidence in her voice, presenting on an object I found very intriguing. And there I was, waiting with sweaty palms to present my sandwich-making robot.

The teacher called on students randomly, so I knew I was up any minute. While I waited to be called on, I spoke to myself to calm myself down. I said: "You'll do fine. There are many students in this class, but most of them are not paying attention. You'll do fine. You have to be up there only for 5 minutes, that is, for 300 seconds. Just focus and get through them. Once you do, you'll resume life as it was before this class."

It seemed to work only temporarily, however. When my teacher called my name, my heart began racing, my hands began to tremble, and my ears began to feel hot. I got up and walked slowly to the front of the class.

I stayed composed while introducing myself, getting through my name and classification with ease. Then, I looked down at my paper as it was facing me and said to myself, "Here we go." I turned my paper around and showed it to the class. On it was a robot, stereotypically designed. Arms, legs, feet, head, chest, and abdomen were drawn with boxes—as every other robot we know is. On its abdomen was a circle representing a hole that fed into the robot's stomach. You guessed it; that is where the robot funneled out the sandwiches to its owner(s) and whoever the owner(s) wanted to feed. Initially, the students reacted with laughter, something that made me feel terribly uncomfortable. I then heard my teacher mumble: "Jesus Christ." The students erupted in even more laughter. My face began to feel swollen and stingingly hot; at that point I knew my face was going to turn red. I tried to keep cool, but I failed. I was embarrassed and ashamed.

My face turned completely red, and I started sweating profusely just underneath my hairline, all across my forehead. To top it off, my mouth dried up so bad I couldn't speak properly, all while my heart kept pounding hard and rapidly.

All eyes were on me. How ironic, I thought. During presentations that were worth their time, students were occupied with something else, looking through their phone. During my presentation, clearly a bad one, all students' attention was on me. I couldn't take it. At about the two and a half minute mark, I looked at my teacher and said I was done and asked if I could be excused. He nodded his head slightly, as if knowing I had the urgency to leave the room because of the breakdown I had suffered. I left the classroom and didn't return to class until the following day.

This is a widely held fear among students, but no student can save himself or herself from it. To succeed, we must be able to present to others on various topics. We cannot hide or runaway from this fear. We must confront it; I'm here to confront it with you It will take time to get over this fear. Just know that it is possible.

Chapter 21: Applying The S.U.C.C.E.S.S Acronym

In the brilliant book **How to Deliver a Great TED Talk** by Akash Karia, Akash applies a strategy for delivering powerful messages first developed by Chip and Dan Heath in **Made to Stick.**

The acronym is a powerful takeaway that builds on other aspects I have talked about. It synergises them in one easy-to-remember format. Let's walk through the elements now.

Simple

The presentation needs to have a simple message. By using the "have a clear focus" chapter of this book, you should be able to hone down your message into something very clear and very simple. Less is more.

Unexpected

By presenting a message that is unexpected, you will ensure a strong emotional reaction from the audience. The sense of "newness" and surprise will mean that the message hits home and is a compelling experience.

Consider also incorporating aspects of the unexpected in how you present your message. This might be a surprising twist in the story you tell, or an unexpected connection that leads you to a new conclusion.

Concrete

Definite, specific messages are better than vague ones. Where possible, move toward ideas and language that have definite dates, numbers, and facts. For example, don't just use the message "How to exercise more." Instead consider something like, "How to put on 2 pounds of muscle in a month." The latter message is better because of the concrete nature of the message.

Credible

Expressing a credible message is essential. To use a variation of the exercise example I began above, "How to put on 2 pounds of muscle tomorrow" is not credible. It just isn't. However, "How to put on 2 pounds of muscle in a month" is credible (though admittedly at the ragged edge of what the fitness community would accept as possible.)

Credibility in your message will sometimes mean a trade-off with a message that sounds more exciting. You want your audience to be a little bit surprised with the message, but they should not dismiss it out of hand for being too unbelievable.

The more ambitious the message you are presenting, the more evidence you will need to show. This evidence might be offered through studies, third party sources, testimonials, etc.

Emotional

A good presentation needs to elicit strong emotions from the audience. Below are some ideas on how to do this:

Story-telling.

Focus on the benefits the audience will experience. "You will live 5 years longer if you exercise by doing X every day" is more emotional because it is benefit-focused. Whereas a message like "Scientists recommend exercise" feels cold and lacks a clear benefit to the audience.

Use emotive language. For example, "I feel amazing when I exercise" is more emotive than "Endorphins are released when humans exercise."

Story

I cover this in detail in the "tell a story" chapter. Story-telling is key to great presentations.

That is it. A simple 6-step overview on how to deliver a fantastic message and give a great presentation.

Business/Problem-Centred Presentations: Apply the "Situation-Complication-Resolution Framework"

The author David McKinsey, in the excellent book **Strategic Storytelling: How to Create Persuasive Business Presentations**, outlines a framework that acts as excellent "training wheels" if you are attempting to solve a problem in your presentation, or if you have a more business-centric presentation.

Barbara Minto was the original creator of this framework, and her contributions to business and business consultancy are well worth researching if this is your field.

Below is a simplified version of the framework. For a simple planning method to create your presentation, use each of the following steps as a section of your presentation. When performing a more complex/business/problem-solving presentation, it can be helpful to adhere to frameworks like this to ensure that you stay focused, on-track, and to keep everyone "on the same page."

Step 1: Identify the problem that you want to solve

Approaching your presentation in terms of problem-solution may itself be an important change in strategy when creating your presentation. But it is also essential that you attempt to solve the **right** problem. McKinsey states the importance of always trying to move "up the issue tree." The closer you get to the core problem, the surer you can be that the problem you are trying to solve is the most critical.

Step 2: Identify constraints

What are the roadblocks to resolving the identified problem? Without knowing what the parameters of the problem are, you won't be able to navigate to the best solution.

Step 3: Lay out all of the involved issues

You should effectively create a map of the terrain that you are going to navigate to get to your solution. This terrain depends entirely on the problem that you are addressing. For example, if the problem you are trying to fix is a new product that isn't selling well, you might list issues such as:

Competition in the product's niche has increased.

We have launched this product at a higher price-point than we normally would.

The product was well-received during market research, so we believe it to be good.

Step 4: Propose answers to the problem

Here, create rigorous action-plans that will solve the problem. Again, this is different from a TED talk. You aren't just going to be engaging and selling an idea; during a problem-solving presentation in "business," you are going to be creating a dialogue, and there will often be many ways to solve a potential problem.

A simple example might be if the problem is dipping profits in the business. In this case, you might propose three answers:

Release a new product

Begin a new ad campaign online

Cut costs by buying more efficient machinery

Step 5: Prioritize your answers

Whoever you are presenting to will want to know which of the solutions are better and why.

McKinsey suggests creating a 2 x 2 grid and using "impact" and "ease of impact" as the two axis headings. He also suggests "fit with values," "strategic alignment," and "fit with capabilities" as possible headings.

However you assess the solutions, the important thing is to assess each solution the same way. You can play each one off against the others to create a list of solutions from "best" to "worst" with reasons why.

Step 6: "Ghost Out" the solution process

It is essential to create a linear process for how the problem will be resolved. Choosing one of the preferred solutions and then applying it to a story board process will help reveal how the solutions will play out.

Doing this process on paper and/or drawing it on-screen can be helpful as you can walk through it step-by-step along with the audience. Stage 1 moves to Stage 2, etc. This is a lot more helpful than jumping around among points, or just showing the entire process all at once on one slide. This is a great time to take feedback and questions from the audience both to help them understand what the proposed solution is and to troubleshoot your own processes. No matter how much prep you do, there is no guarantee that the solution you want to propose won't be easily shot down by someone who has specialized knowledge of the field.

Step 7: Test Your solutions, get feedback, and iterate your story

Seeing your presentation as part of an ongoing process is important to its overall effectiveness. Once you have chosen the best solution and it is being implemented, you will need to assess how well the solution is working. Course-correct, and get feedback. Return to this process if more problems come up, and be sure to return to the notes of your presentation to remind yourself of the problem-resolution process you/the business decided on.

McKinsey states the importance of feedback from all of the key members who are involved in the problem and the implementation of the solution. He suggests ensuring that these are done in cycles as part of an ongoing process of improving the business.

Final Ideas on this Framework

This framework will be most helpful for readers who are trying to solve problems and those giving presentations in a business/corporate setting. If you are giving a more relaxed, entertaining presentation or perhaps presenting as part of an education course, this framework might have sounded a little too rigid and dry. However, even in these cases, consider the following to glean help from this framework:

An overall process/framework to your presentation brings clarity and structure to your presentation.

Many presentations can be boiled down to a problem-solution format. Try doing this with your presentation to help your own understanding of the message you are conveying.

The problem-solution format is very compelling to an audience – don't we all want answers to life's problems? So if you can reform or adapt your presentation into this model (perhaps minus the rigid framework above), you might make your presentation more effective.

Chapter 22: Maintain Your Focus On The Subject Matter, Not The Audience

This may seem like common sense however many people get so wrapped up in the audience (particularly if it is a big audience they are talking to) that they lose focus on their material. Maintain focus on the content and delivery of your speech. As you practice getting excited this issue will slowly resolve on its own, however it is an important point to make in general. If you are anxious, it is only natural that your attention will be drawn to the audience. Think back to our discussion regarding the brain. If your amygdala is worried about something, it will make darn sure you focus on it! So use your conscious brain to bring your attention back to the material and away from the audience. Think of it like a mindfulness meditation exercise. When you find your attention drifting towards the audience, gently bring it back to the material.

Getting momentarily stuck or appearing a little nervous is not the end of the world

Don't seek perfection. Even the world's greatest orators (such as Barack Obama) make mistakes. Plan to get stuck, lose your train of thought, say the wrong word, and mispronounce a word here and there. It's perfectly normal. The audience will never thing poorly of you for making a mistake. Remember, the audience is usually on your side (a hostile audience is probably not within the scope of this book as that requires an entirely different approach) so they are not taking pleasure in each little mistake. In fact, if you appear a little nervous (it may take one or two goes to perfect your excitement strategy) you may even garner additional empathy from the audience which will work in your favour.

Break the tension with humour

This is one of my secret strategies which is amazingly effective. Before any presentation, I ensure that I have a chance to talk one on one with some of the people in the audience or make a small joke as I am getting prepared to speak. This is incredibly effective because it sends the signal to your brain that yes, this is something exciting and fun — not something which requires vigilance and anxiety. If you make a small joke or a light-hearted comment, it breaks all the tension and almost as if by magic, transforms any anxiety into excitement.

Act like a professional athlete

Get into the habit of psyching yourself up rather than trying to calm yourself down before a speech. Don't be afraid to say a few "C'mons!" inside your head (or even out aloud if you can find somewhere to be alone). Picture yourself as a boxer before a fight or a tennis player before a big final. As long as no one is around, I like to do a couple of playful punches and muscle stretches as I pretend to be a boxer before a fight. Just make sure you are out of sight. You don't want the audience to think that you're a weirdo!

You never look as nervous as you think you do

Back in the day before I discovered this technique, many times I was a nervous wreck before my speech and was sure that it was a disaster, only to have people truthfully tell me I didn't even look nervous! Take solace in the fact that, irrespective of how you feel, only the most extreme of nerves will even be noticeable. Below a certain threshold it just looks as if you are aroused appropriately. After all, as I mentioned earlier, people prefer someone who looks a little keyed up rather than an almost sedated zombie!

Toastmasters

Toastmasters is a large non-profit organisation dedicated to teaching the art of public speaking. I strongly urge you to seek out your local chapter and join up for several reasons. Firstly, Toastmasters provides you with a fantastic environment to perfect your speaking skills amongst likeminded others. Secondly, it is consistent with my previous advice to actively seek out speaking engagements. By proactively joining Toastmasters and giving presentations, you are gradually training your amygdala to view public speaking as something you approach, rather than something you escape from. This will accelerate the process of viewing public speaking as something genuinely exciting.

Chapter 23: Public Speaking Is Easy When You Know What To Say!

If one of your fears is that you are not quite sure what to say to your audience, then again this is not a problem once you have been doing the exercises and changing your mental attitude as you have been reading thus far.

Remember when I asked you earlier to do a simple 100-word speech on cheese? How did you do? If I were to ask you to do some research on this commonplace item, do you think you would learn something new about cheese? I am sure you would learn something new! Your audience always wants to hear something new. You do become a bore of a speaker when spend precious minutes telling an audience what they already know. When you are an interested person, you become an **interesting** speaker – which is critically important for you to become a habitual reader and word searcher – and yes, you may do this in a fun manner!

The type of speeches you have to make will certainly depend on the occasion. The formality of the speech will determine your content; if the speech is informal then speech content would suit the occasion. What a disaster it would be to have the wrong content on the wrong occasion!

Let us define what type of speeches fall within two main categories to help us to understand how to build content for our speeches.

FORMAL SPEECHES

Formal speeches are held every day, on many different occasions. We attend these occasions via our televisions almost on a daily basis, so we are constantly being exposed to the formal occasions taking place around the world.

The following are examples of occasions for formal speeches:

Awards Functions

Business presentations

Conferences

Debates

Funerals

Graduation

Head of State Address

Weddings

The type of occasion determines the speech content that is required for your presentation.

INFORMAL SPEECHES

Informal speeches tend to be more common than formal speeches, but nevertheless entail the same kinds of requirements as formal speech, but without the protocols. Informal speeches may be distinguished by the conversational tones, use of colloquial and slang language; informal speeches may be impromptu speeches, toasts, introductions, and the like.

You still can afford to create a favourable impression in these informal settings, as they could lead to opportunities in formal occasions.

Occasions for informal speeches include:

Fun & games night

Family occasion

Engagement, birthday, retirement, parties

FORMAL SPEECH CONTENT

In a formal speech delivery, an audience seeks new information, authenticity, integrity, intelligence, discipline, wit, humour (where necessary), valid facts, even a little controversy to cause new thinking. As a speaker at a formal event you need to first of all observe the appropriate protocol of address; in preparation you must always find out what protocol applies in the situation, because it may vary depending on the hosting of the event. Protocol observes the hierarchy and honour of special guests, giving them their due recognition on the occasion; it also informs other members of the audience about who is present amongst them at the event.

To be professional in a formal speech delivery, make sure your content contains at least three major points. Always make sure to do your research ahead of time to add appropriate information to your speech presentation. Explain these major points in detail using appropriate examples, stories, anecdotes, jokes, statistics, or little known facts. Be familiar with your content; choose what you enjoy sharing.

If there is an area that goes against your views or understanding do not struggle with it, find something else that you are far more comfortable with.

Always begin with an introduction, which gives the audience an idea of what to expect so they can follow your presentation; next, present the body of your speech with your main points, complete with the explanations and finally deliver the conclusion of your presentation. Your conclusion reiterates your introduction, causes your audience to take action where necessary or by their applause you can tell whether you have made a connection with your audience. If you desire the audience to act in a particular way their response will also demonstrate the impact that you have had.

All speeches have a structure: ***introduction, body and conclusion***. You have as much latitude as ever to create an exciting speech presentation. Share your writing with a genuine friend or mentor.

INFORMAL SPEECH CONTENT

The content for informal speech follows the same format of introduction, body and conclusion.

The difference between a formal speech and informal speech is the degree of familiarity with your audience and your comfort with the occasion. This means you have to be comfortable with yourself, and have a willingness to be candid on the spur of the moment. The comfort with yourself will come from all the exercises I have shared with you throughout the book.

The main point of an informal speech is that it is usually very short, witty and carries good feelings towards all.

Once you have ideas, thoughts and opinions you do have something to share – formally or informally. You can do it!

Chapter 24: Persuasive Speaking

We are persuading and persuading very day. We may even be persuaded almost every moment of every day, depending on what we do. Think about your day. Here is a little snapshot of mine:

When I wake up and get ready for my day I often turn on the TV to see the weather and catch up on news. When I do that, I see commercials. Sometimes I act on them. Then, I log onto my computer and I check my Facebook page. Ahhh---there they are again: messages, ads. suggestions on stuff to buy! Sometimes I act on them. Then, I get in my car and I turn on my radio – even if it is NPR there are program sponsors –messages—that try to convince me to think about organizations in different ways. And, even when I don't see ads, I am persuaded by information I see and hear. A favorite actress looks particularly great in a blue dress. I find myself wanting a blue dress. A person I admire tells me about a new restaurant, a new book, or a new smart phone app and I want them all. Information and persuasion. They are clearly on a continuum.

Persuasive speaking can be contrasted with informative speaking.

Informative ---------------------- Persuasive

There are several points of contrast:

1. Persuasive speaking urges us to choose from among options: informative speaking reveals and clarifies options.

2. Persuasive speaking asks the audience for more commitment than does informative speaking.

3. The ethical obligations for persuasive speakers are even greater than for informative speakers.

4. The Persuasive speaker is an opinion leader; the informative speaker is a teacher.

5. Persuasive speaking more often involves emotional appeals that are out of place in speeches to inform.

Focuses of Persuasion

Question of fact:

This refers to something that we can know to be either true or false, but right now we can argue about it. Examples include historical controversy, predictions, or questions of existence. Examples: "To persuade my audience that vegetarians live longer than meat eaters." "To persuade my audience that global warming is happening in America." "To persuade my audience that Apple stock prices will continue to rise."

Question of value:

Here is where we argue something is right or wrong, moral or immoral, or better or worse than another thing. Examples include: "To persuade my audience that it is wrong to use social networking at work." "To persuade my audience that hybrid cars are better than gasoline based vehicles." "To persuade my audience that it is better to take out loans and earn a college degree than have no degree at all."

Question of policy:

Here is where we argue that some action should or should not be taken.

The form is always: "To persuade my audience that X should do Y."

"To persuade my audience that Lance Armstrong should be stripped of all his titles." "To persuade my audience that Congress should make a law that requires gender parity in elections." "To persuade my audience that people should stop buying sugary soft drinks."

There are four common goals of persuasion:

To reinforce the beliefs and attitudes that already exist

To change attitudes

To guard or inoculate against counter-persuasion

To cause the audience to take action

Greek philosophers identified several persuasive measures: Ethos, Pathos, Logos

Ethos is an appeal to the authority or honesty of the presenter. It is how well the presenter convinces the audience that he or she is qualified to present (speak) on the particular subject. It can be done in many ways:

By being a notable figure in the field in question, such as a medical doctor reporting on medical breakthroughs, for example Dr. Sanjay Gupta of CNN.

When he speaks about the harmfulness of not getting a flu shot his credibility as a doctor (or ethos) comes into play.

As a persuasive speaker you must ask yourself:

"What am I a credible spokesperson for?"

What do I know about and will people believe me to be knowledgable about? It is why cyclist Lance Armstrong has lost his credibility in a lot of people's eyes. He lied about using performance enhancement drugs so many people no longer believe anything he says is true.

Pathos is an appeal to the audience's emotions. It can be in the form of metaphor, simile, a passionate delivery, or even a simple claim that a matter is unjust. Pathos can be particularly powerful if used well, but most speeches do not solely rely on pathos. Pathos is most effective when the author or speaker demonstrates agreement with an underlying value of the reader or listener.

In addition, the speaker may use pathos to appeal to fear, in order to sway the audience. Pathos may also include appeals to audience imagination and hopes; done when the speaker paints a scenario of positive future results of following the course of action proposed.

Logos is logical appeal or the simulation of it, and the term logic is derived from it. It is normally used to describe facts and figures that support the speaker's topic. Having a logos appeal also enhances ethos because information makes the speaker look knowledgeable and prepared to his or her audience. However, the data can be confusing and thus confuse the audience. Logos can also be misleading or inaccurate, however meaningful it may seem to the subject at hand. In some cases, inaccurate, falsified, or miscontextualized data can even be used to enact a pathos effect.

Source credibility (ethos) is composed of competence and character. The elaboration likelihood model reflects two potential paths an audience can take in response to a persuasive message:

Central route processing involves elaborated and critical thinking.

Peripheral route processing relies on cues, such as emotional appeals.

Evidence can greatly enhance a persuasive presentation. Three types of evidence are:
first-order data: personal experience
second-order data: expert testimony
third-order data: facts and statistics
Two-sided messages are generally more effective than one-sided speeches:
Two-sided messages confer greater credibility.
Two-sided messages help inoculate an audience against counter-persuasion.
Peripheral cues include emotions such as fear and primitive beliefs about:
reciprocity
liking
authority
social support
scarcity
Use of support material constitutes offering "good reasons" to accept a claim.
Three Types of Support Material
Examples
Statistics

Testimony

All three types of support material require that you:

make accurate use

evaluate and identify the source (beware bias)

consider the currency of the material (is it too old to be accurate?)

consider strength

Tips for effective use of examples:

1. Do not use them alone to support an important claim.

2. Examples are useful in clarifying, reinforcing, or personalizing ideas.

3 Ethical use demands that you consider the source, age, and representativeness of the example.

Tips for effective use of statistics:

1. Combine statistics with examples.

2. Don't use too many at a time.

3. Identify the source of the statistics.

4. Translate your statistics.

5. Round off your statistics.

6. Use visual aids.

Tips for effective use of testimony:

1. Quote accurately.
2. Paraphrase fairly.
3. Use qualified sources.
4. Use reluctant testimony.
5. Always identify the source and the source's credentials.

Methods of Persuasion: Reasoning

The two main forms of reasoning are deduction and induction.

A. Deduction refers to arguments that run from general to specific; they are characterized by necessity.

B. Induction refers to arguments that run from specific to general; they are characterized by an inductive leap.

Classic form of Deduction: the syllogism

The U.S. Constitution guarantees citizens the right to vote.

Women are citizens.

**The U.S. Constitution guarantees women the right to vote.

Senator Grassley has recently argued:

What is good for Farmers is good for Iowa.

The chapter 12 bankruptcy provision is good for farmers.

Therefore, the chapter q2 bankruptcy provision is good for Iowa

Popular form of Deduction: The Enthymeme:

George Bush is not a wimp; he's a military hero.

She's a girl; she can't throw the ball.

He's a man, of course he wouldn't stop to ask directions.

Our text associates deductive reasoning with the class of arguments called arguments from principle.

In the Chewing Tobacco Speech:

To be effective a law must be enforced and have adequate penalties.

Adopting my plan will make Wisconsin's laws on chewing tobacco be enforced and will create adequate penalties.

My plan will be effective at curbing chewing tobacco use.

Beware the false principle.

The police say he committed the crime, so he committed the crime.

stereotypes

starting from principles that only those who already agree with you would maintain.

The major form of Inductive reasoning our text calls argument from specific instances.

[Otherwise known as generalization arguments.]

In the chewing tobacco speech:

"Chewing tobacco use is widespread."

Proof

The American Cancer Society says one in twelve Americans is a regular user.

The average age of first use is 10.

40% of high school boys say they have tried it.

21% of kindergartners (boys?) have tried it.

Surveys, studies, and even elections are often grounded in reasoning from specific instances.

conducting a poll

"Four out of five dentists surveyed"

Nielsen ratings

Beware the Hasty Generalization

my friends and I watched violent cartoons and never committed a crime, so . . . .

the two people I sat next to in lecture got Bs on their speeches, so everybody but me got a B on the speech.

"but Mom, everybody else is going to the party!"

Arguments from Analogy

Literal and Figurative; both are grounded in the concept of similarity

Literal Analogies

Socialized medicine works in Canada, so socialized medicine will work in the U.S.

The U.S. got rid of the half-penny in 1857 without causing harms, so today we can get rid of the penny without causing harms.

Higher penalties for selling chewing tobacco to minors in California has reduced chewing tobacco use by minors by 60%. Therefore, higher penalties in Wisconsin will also work.

The Kansas City Royals have switched from chewing tobacco to bubble gum, so other teams would switch if people appealed to them.

Weak Analogies

Having a funeral without the body is like having a wedding without the bride.

The university shouldn't be able to tell me what classes I have to take; after all, the store manager doesn't tell me what groceries to buy.

A ban on all alcohol use in the dorms will work at ISU because such a ban worked at Simpson College.

Figurative Analogies

useful for framing an argument

As the tiger needs its claws to provide for its internal needs, so does America need its defense in order to meet domestic concerns.

Malcolm X: An integrated civil rights movement is like strong black coffee diluted with cream; its strength is lost.

Causal Arguments

The most challenging of the types of reasoning. We can't see causal relationships, we can only infer them.

Hume saw that in order to conclude a causal relationship we must see constant conjunctions as well as a relationship in time. Furthermore, the causal link must make "sense" according to our sense of how the world works.

How do we reach the conclusion that cigarettes cause lung cancer?

Problems of Causal Arguments

"post hoc ergo propter hoc" = "after this therefore because of this"

It happens when we leap from a simple relationship in time to a belief in a causal link with insufficient support. Superstitions are classic cases of the post hoc fallacy. It is also seen in "just look what happened after we .... " arguments.

Multiple Causation

The problem arises when we fail to acknowledge that causal relationships are often quite complicated. To baldly assert: "rain forest destruction is the cause of global warming," is to invite an audience to argue with you mentally as they list the other causes they have heard discussed. Again, to claim: "T.V. is responsible for school gun violence" will require much discussion and evidence and will be better handled if you acknowledge that there are multiple factors that contribute. Then you can focus on the one source of the problem and the solutions to it.

correlation vs. causation

Did you know that every year as the amount of ice cream being eaten in this country increases, so do the number of drownings?

Tips for success in causal reasoning.

use causal chains to help the audience see the causal relationship.

use testimony of experts to support conclusions

PERSUASIVE ORGANIZATIONAL PATTERNS

For your persuasive speeches, you may select from the following organizational patterns below. In any case, choose the pattern that best fits your audience and your topic.

I. Statement of Reasons Method

If your audience has no opinion on the subject, are not interested, or only mildly in favor or against your proposition. This speech is most effective in speeches to stimulate.

With this particular pattern each reason is presented as a complete statement arguing for your proposition. You mainly concentrate on the advantages of your proposition. For example, if you were giving a speech persuading us to vote, your main points might look like this:

1. Voting will allow you to contribute to the democratic process.
2. Voting will allow you to voice your views on many important issues.
3. Voting will increase your social and political awareness.

II. Problem –Solution

This pattern provides you with a strategy of clarifying the nature of the problem, offering your proposal, and illustrating why your proposal is the best one. If you use this pattern you must address all four areas.

1. Problem Is there a significant problem with ¼

What are the signs of the problem?

What is the specific harm?
How widespread is the harm?

2. Blame Is the current system of solving the problem
incapable or to blame for the problem?
What causes the problem?
Is the present system at fault?
Should the present system be changed?

3. Solution Will the proposed policy solve or significantly reduce the problem?
What are the possible solutions?
Which solution best solves the problem?

4. Cost Will the benefits of solving the problem outweigh the costs of implementing the solution?
What good outcomes will result?
What bad outcomes will result?

III. Monroe's Motivated Sequence

1. Attention – Wow Us!
2. Need – you need to make the audience concerned with your problem.

Support with evidence.

3. Satisfaction – Provide a solution to satisfy the need.

4. Visualization – the audience needs to visualize the benefits of the plan. Bespecific and apply it to your audience.

5. Action – Call to action – tell the audience what you want them to do and how they can do it. Be specific!

IF YOUR ADUIENCE IS OPPOSED TO OR HOSTILE TO YOUR PROPOSITION USE

IV. Criteria Satisfaction Method

This pattern focuses on developing a yes-response from your audience before you introduce your proposition and reasons. Having established a criteria in you first point, you argue in your second point that your proposition satisfies that criteria. This pattern is most effective in speeches to convince and actuate. For example, if you wanted your audience to vote for a hike in school taxes, your main points might look like this:

1. We all want good schools.

a. Good schools have programs that prepare our youth to function effectively in society.

b. Good schools are those with the best teachers available.

2. Passing the proposed school tax will guarantee good schools.

a. Passing the tax will increase the quality of vital programs.

b. Passing the tax will enable us to hire and keep the best teachers.

V. Negative Method

With this method you focus on the shortcomings of all the potential solutions to a problem except the one offered by you. After you have dealt with the other potential solutions you offer your proposition. This speech is most effective in speeches to actuate. For example, if you wanted to persuade your audience that the Serbian war crimes must be stopped, you argument might look like this:

1. The UN will not solve this problem.

2. Negotiations between Croatia, Serbia and Bosnia will not solve the problem.

3. Direct negotiations by the US will not solve the problem.

4. The only way to solve the problem effectively is to send troops into the former Yugoslavia.

Conlusion

Public speaking is an impressive art of communication with the audience in a structured and deliberate manner. It goes beyond the boundaries of speaking or talking to a group of individuals. It is an art of articulating your ideas and thoughts in order to persuade others, inspire them, engage them, or entertain them.

There are three main components of public speaking - logical component, mechanical component, and emotional component. A good and effective speech should have a merger of all these three components.

Logical component attributes to the content of your speech that encompasses the truth and facts you deliver along with the structure ad length of your speech. The content or the material of your speech should be engaging, entertaining, as well as inspiring.

Mechanical component caters to your tone of voice and your body movements. When you change the tone of your voice or make any unexpected body movements notice how your audience perceives your speech. This perception will define the success or failure of your speech.

The emotional component attributes to the emotions you deliver during your speech and how the audience feels after your speech. These emotions should be strong enough to directly affect the way audience feel and further convince them to put your words into actions.

Apart from these components there are various factors that influence this art of communication. Some of these factors include your level of confidence, facial expressions, catchy titles, rate of speech, usage of visual aids, and the usage of entertaining or captivating stuff like true stories, real life experiences, jokes, or phrases.

Furthermore, you should very well know the content of your speech so that you can make eye contact with the audience and deliver your message in a lively and convincing manner.

Take a deep breath before you start your speech as this will help you gain control over your nerves, your voice, and your words as well. Keep your mind and heart open and feel relaxed. Eye contact is really important in public speaking as it is the best way to express your emotions and impress the audience. Even if you are nervous appear as if things are normal and there is nothing wrong at your end. Pass a smile when you feel tensed as this will ease your mind and keep you in comfort.

You should also have a good sense of humor. Wherever possible tell funny jokes and lighten the mood of people or tell stories from real life or personal experience to add life and energy to your speech. In all possible ways try to engage the audience till the end of your speech by finding different ways to humanize your speech. Last but not the least, there are situations where you make mistakes but there is nothing to worry. Human make mistakes but what is important is how these mistakes are recovered.

It's fun, energetic, and great to empower this art of public speaking as it has its own set of benefits and advantages. It helps you increase your self-confidence, increase your motivation power, boost your career graph, and even improve your quality of life.

Whatever your reason of fearing public speaking, I strongly urge you to overcome your fear and do public speaking. Someone smart said "A life lived in fear is a life half lived." I totally agree. If you are going to let your fears force you not to become a public speaker, then you are missing out big time.

Public speaking is fun. Yes, it is nerve racking and strenuous and often difficult, but it a lot of fun. I cannot highlight how satisfying it feels having hundreds of people laugh or cry or do whenever you want. (Maybe I am just a control freak!)

And of course, having those hundreds of people give you a big round of applause at the end of your presentation is a moment that I recommend all to experience. To have individuals come up and say "That speech was the best I have heard in years" or "That speech changed my life" or even having complete strangers come up and say "Thank you, that was great" - it doesn't get any better than that.

Don't let your fears stop you being a public speaker.

www.ingramcontent.com/pod-product-compliance
Lightning Source LLC
Chambersburg PA
CBHW072005070526
44583CB00015B/1344